the myrtlewood cookbook

Pacific Northwest Home Cooking

Andrew Barton

PHOTOGRAPHY BY Peter Schweitzer

Styling by Kate Schweitzer

SASQUATCH BOOKS

SEATTLE

CONTENTS

RECIPES

INTRODUCTION

How This Book Came to Be

I am a preschool teacher. I have never worked in a restaurant.

Less than a year after graduating college, I started a monthly supper club called Secret Restaurant Portland. Back then it was slightly more ragtag, but the spirit remains the same today. We cook seasonal meals created spontaneously and collaboratively, using whatever ingredients are most directly available to us or are currently inspiring our creativity. We do this for no profit—just the love of cooking and creating memorable experiences.

Once this project was fully underway, cooking became an increasingly serious occupation of mine. I began reading cookbooks every night before bed and collecting kitchen equipment. I was shopping with a keener, more focused eye and thinking about gardening. Soon I had a large garden, some foraging experience, several annual food-related rituals, and a website to document the meals I'd been making. I became a true cook by approaching cooking with wonder, aplomb, humor, and joy.

One day, riding the bus or walking to the co-op, I decided to make a cookbook with Peter and Kate Schweitzer. We'd already been working together for years on the Secret Restaurant project. I cook with Lucas Winiarski and Sofie Sherman-Burton—the greatest kitchen comrades—and the Schweitzers help behind the scenes. They jump in with last-minute prep, often create the table settings and dining atmosphere, and always capture the event with their beautiful pictures. I had to ask nicely about the book project, but they weren't too hard to convince.

We spent a year and a half, almost exactly, shooting every week or two for the book. Peter and Kate would come over to my home kitchen where I'd usually have about three-quarters of the cooking done, working alone with the tape deck on. They would help me finish prepping and organizing, then we would shoot each dish one at a time. After shooting we would sit down to enjoy the meal, sometimes with friends and roommates joining in. Often we'd plan the next phase as we ate, before tidying up. Then they would go home and I'd pick my life up right where I'd left it before switching on the tape deck several hours earlier.

The recipes in this book are about my tastes, family traditions, loved ones, home, places visited, and the region where I live. The food you cook can do this too! Think about your favorite things to eat or your favorite things from childhood, make some lists, and start learning to cook them or to cook them better. Mark the recipes in this book that most appeal to you and dive in! Do that with your other cookbooks too. Cooking can be about just getting fed, but it should often be about learning how to make new things and getting closer to mastering your favorites. Start to tweak recipes to your own taste, then challenge yourself to make something you've never been served before.

This book was originally self-published, funded by a Kickstarter campaign in 2015. It was shot, written, edited, and designed entirely independently. The first edition was printed in Portland, Oregon, and distributed in select cities. It sold out within six months. We are thrilled to be working with Sasquatch Books and sharing this new edition with a wider audience. We hope the book finds its place by your bedside, in your backpack, or on the kitchen counter.

The Name

Myrtlewood is the name of a rare bay laurel tree, which only grows in Northern California and Oregon.

The leaves can be used in the kitchen the same way as bay leaves. The wood from the tree is a prized wood for making plates, cutting boards, and bowls. In the early to mid-twentieth century, there was a large trade of myrtlewood souvenirs in Oregon. Over the last few years, if I encountered myrtlewood pieces I could actually use in the kitchen at a good price, I would collect them.

Researching further, I found that the tree first appears on the Oregon coast, near Florence. Florence is the coastal town most parallel to my hometown of Eugene. My book found a name in a tree I'd grown up near, which thrives in the land I continue to live in, and now has a treasured place in my kitchen.

I remember the countertop bookshelf in the kitchen of my childhood home where the *Moosewood Cookbook* and *The Enchanted Broccoli Forest* by Mollie Katzen stood side by side. Earthy, vegetable-focused recipes from these books made their way into our family's rotation of favorites. I would see my mom take the books down from their familiar spot, bust out a delicious savory pie, and put them back again. One day as a slouching, thrift-store-plaid-wearing teenager, I finally pulled the books down myself. With the book on my lap and a tub of hummus and a bag of tortilla chips precariously balanced, I flew through *Moosewood* like it was a hot new page-turner. Over the next year, my mother and I made it through a number of recipes, and by the end of college, I'm pretty sure I'd cooked the whole book.

My folks sent me to college with a copy of my own. I added it to our collection at my co-op house, and it was used more than any other cookbook. When I returned after the first summer, the copy was gone, and I was quietly distraught. But on a golden-sunshine autumn afternoon while walking toward campus, I noticed the annual book sale at the village library. The handwritten spine of *Moosewood* was recognizable from ten feet away, at the bottom of a stack. It was an earlier edition than any I'd seen before, the cover torn slightly from the spine. I lovingly repaired it with masking tape, and have held onto it dearly ever since.

Gardening

After abandoning ambitions to move to New Hampshire and start a farm with college friends, I created an urban garden in the unused lot next to my house. My grandparents were farmers and I felt the biological urge to garden, but until then I'd barely set a hand in the dirt. It was a very large and ambitious project for a first-time grower, but by doing my reading and having knowledge-able, helpful friends, the garden came together beautifully. I learned so much that growing year, cooking everything I grew with a new reverence.

The following winter, the garden was destroyed and the lot turned into cheaply made condos. Determined not to give up my beautiful gardening and cooking setup, I found a fallow space across the street that was no longer tended by anyone. My neighbors had inherited the space as-is when they started to rent there and agreed to let me garden in exchange for basic yard maintenance outside the cultivated beds. There are three fenced-in areas in the lot, which now contain fourteen garden beds and a container garden. Already established but in need of some love were raspberry canes, a kiwi bush, some hop vines, an apple tree, two cherry trees, and the ubiquitous blackberry brambles. I am incredibly lucky to have bumbled upon this secret garden.

It took two seasons and the help of many friends to establish all the new growing spaces and to shift my backyard into a productive greens garden (shade from the surrounding developments made very little else possible). Now I tend these spaces on my own. It is hard to balance with teaching work and other projects, but it is worth it to be able to grow a wide variety of vegetables and fruits within a few hundred feet of my kitchen.

It would be absurd to expect everyone to do the same thing, but I urge every reader to find some deeper connection to your food! Start going to the same stand at your farmers' market every week, so you can see how their growing year goes. Pay closer attention to the little signs in the produce section at the natural foods market or co-op. Start some herbs in pots on your window sill or your front stoop. Plant one row of lettuces in a friend's garden. Get a small community plot. Dig up that sunny patch of your yard that hasn't been used for anything in years. Get a group of friends together to tackle a larger garden project together. If you can go out on your rooftop, you could probably find a way to grow something up there.

Think of each section of the calendar when your favorite produce is really in season as the time to celebrate it—the growing, the picking, taking it home in your market basket, eating it raw while looking at the sky, or cooking it in a deep pan with lots of butter. Think of these fruits and vegetables as treasures.

Foraging

If you live anywhere near any wild foods, consider learning more about them. Learn what the mushrooms, the nettles, the miner's lettuce, the chickweed, the ramps, and the fiddlehead ferns look like. Investigate where they might be found. Get a group of friends together and pile into the car on a weekend morning. Pack baskets and gloves. Start early. Bring coffee. Plan out the rural or suburban lunch stop you'll make on the way home. Be okay with not finding anything. Be thrilled when you do find something, and celebrate it in your kitchen.

Cast of Characters

Every cook has influences, usually very strong ones, and I think we should wear them proudly on our sleeves.

These are the direct influences of mine who appear in this book.

- Sofie, my partner, who cooks with me more than anyone else. Our story could be told in chapters on cooking and dining, from that late night in the diner when we both put black pepper in the ketchup to the basted eggs and smashed potatoes we had last week. During the creation of this book, she was an endless source of ideas, inspiration, and support.

- My father, who doesn't really know how to cook but sure as hell knows how to write. His dedication to thorough scholarship (he never just dabbles), his devotion to sharing knowledge (teaching college theatre for decades, writing numerous textbooks on theatre), and his boundless belief in me inspired this work.

- My mother, whose no-frills handiwork and strong, simple flavor combinations made me excited to sit down to dinner every night. She taught me to flavor a dish with nothing but celery, she taught me about Old Bay, she taught me that a lumpy cookie with walnuts is often the best cookie.

- My grandmother, whose hamburger gravy with creamed potatoes was the first dish I puzzled over, dreamed about, salivated at the mere thought of, and whose sandwich buns with wheat germ made anything stuffed between the dining event of the century. When I was 12 or 13, shortly before she passed away, she taught me how to make a few of these things.

- Lucas, my childhood friend, who has done Secret Restaurant Portland with me from the beginning. Lucas has an openness and wide-eyed wonder in the kitchen, which makes us work so well as cooking partners. He also has an inclination towards scientific precision (he works as an engineer), and I am grateful to have miraculously absorbed a little of this over time.

- Aria, my partner of many years and good friend, who has taught me so much about wild foods, about gardening, about plant life, about living in the natural world. I'm inspired by her knack for both creating and capturing beauty in her surroundings.

- Asher, my best friend from college. We've met up for adventures often motivated by or punctuated with food every year since. We have been each other's trusted advisor for a decade now. I wouldn't be the person that I am without his wonderful, wise influence.

- Kate, the stylist of this book, whose sense of humor got me through a long stretch of teaching together, and whose friendship has been a monumental joy. Her keen eye helped the pages of this book look as beautiful as they do, and her drive kept the project on course through any and all obstacles.

- Peter, the photographer of this book. He took photos of my food on the day we met, and it was like he'd known me all my life. His open-minded approach and dedication to his craft has inspired me to treat cooking the same way. Working together is like having a friend in the kitchen, because it's exactly that, and I couldn't think of a better way to work.

Kitchen Tools

A GOOD APRON

Find the apron that is right for your body and the way you cook, and wear it every time.

BOWLS

Unequivocally, the kitchen item I use the most is basic, beautiful, and essential—the bowl. A stack of thin metal bowls ranging from enormous to just slightly bigger than a soup bowl, ceramic mixing bowls, bowls made by friends, tiny barely there bowls, wooden serving bowls, wooden soup and cereal bowls . . .

Whenever cooking in someone else's kitchen, I ask how many bowls they have. Why so many bowls? When you have the power to separate out all the elements of the dish or of the meal as a whole, you have a very clear control. In several cases, the time an ingredient spends in a lemon bath or light pickling liquid or marinade is the step that makes the dish, that makes the meal.

Thin metal bowls are the cheapest and the easiest to keep clean, and they never cause a moment's worry. They can be collected at restaurant supply stores or just picked up one at a time in thrift stores.

CAST-IRON PANS

I have one cast-iron combo-cooker, a Dutch oven made up of two pans (a deep-rimmed pan and a standard frying pan) that lid one another. These two serve nearly all of my cooking needs, and a Dutch oven is the ideal tool for baking crusty bread at home.

The pan I find indispensable is a thinner, wider, barely lipped cast-iron griddle pan. It heats up a lot quicker than the thicker pans and is perfect for blasting the moisture out of mushrooms or eggplant. It also works phenomenally well for pancakes, tortillas, and grilled sandwiches.

I also have the classic smaller cast-iron frying pan. This is useful not only for eggs, but also because of its edge designed for pouring, for making small portions of garlic butter, or perhaps fried shallots, to toss over another dish at the last minute.

DIGITAL SCALE

I first bought a digital scale for home bread baking. Shortly after, I started using it every day to measure coffee beans for single cup pour-overs. Then I started using it often for baking, and then for recipes written by British and European writers. After a little while, I was using it to compose new dishes, having internalized some ratios and seeing how well its precision had affected my cooking. Many of the recipes in this book include metric measurements. The scale is a cheap gadget that will change your cooking life.

FISH SPATULA

My fish spatula is in fact not a fish spatula at all, but a tool that looks exactly like a fish spatula labeled "Batter Beater," perhaps made for the '50s housewife who put pancakes on the table every weekday morning.

I have used it nearly every day since finding it at a thrift store the week my first Portland roommates were moving out and taking the kitchen tools with them.

The curved edge, the spaces between the metal lines, the graceful handle. It is truly an extension of your hand, doing most anything you want it to. Lift something out of poaching liquid or frying oil? Check. Flip the egg at the perfect moment? Check. Gracefully crisp the outer skin of a whole trout? Check. Agitate the pile of half melting, half sticking vegetables in a roasting tin? Check. It really does it all.

Even if you can't find or don't want to bother with a fish spatula, find a metal spatula that is thin and flexible enough to actually work. Clumsy plastic or composite spatulas don't make any sense but are in kitchens everywhere.

KIWI KNIVES

Nearly all of my knives are from the Thai brand Kiwi, bought at Asian markets around Oregon (they can also be ordered online). They have attractive, durable wooden handles with blades of quality stainless steel that are razor sharp when new and easy to keep sharp at home. They have the perfect weight and balance. Once you get used to them, you'll hardly ever reach for another. They are also exceedingly affordable. I've given several basic Kiwi chef's knives as gifts. Each time, I later hear that the simple addition of these knives has changed the recipient's cooking life.

MORTAR AND PESTLE

I struggled to successfully use a small mortar and pestle for years, never said anything about it, and only pretended that I liked using it. Then one day, visiting my folks, I remembered the giant mortar and pestle in the upstairs attic room. It had spent my entire youth living on a pedestal in a corner up there. I asked my mom about it and learned that it was my great grandfather's. He was a homeopathic doctor and had used it for his practice. Now it is the most revered item in my kitchen. I crush garlic cloves into paste, smash walnuts for cakes, pound oil and milk into salt cod, get the perfect consistency of cardamom (some whole bits and some near powder), make my own spice mixes for Indian food, and so much more.

NONSTICK PAN

One stick-resistant pan that heats up quickly is essential. I have one thin but very sturdy old Farberware pan, found at a garage sale long ago. It doesn't flake and deteriorate like teflon, and fills any need I might have for a nonstick pan.

REVERE WARE POTS

I grew up with a Revere Ware tea kettle and assorted saucepans. Now I have some for myself—one came from a yard sale, one from my mother, and one was left behind by a former roommate. I truly appreciate their classic perfection. The control of the heat you get from the copper bottom, the closely fitting lids, the drastic variety of sizes! They are too accessible, and too wonderful to not have a small collection. They will serve you well.

ROASTING TINS

I love my collection of banged-up roasting tins, all found by chance, already extremely worn in, or given to me by friends who know how much I love roasting tins and their various patinas. Start a collection for yourself!

SOUP POT OR LARGER DUTCH OVEN

Every kitchen should have a large durable, "never going to fail" pot. I have yet to find my dream enamel cast-iron Le Creuset or equivalent, so I just use the heavy-bottomed, lidded, made-in-the-USA-at-some-point-in-the-past pot that I found for three dollars at a garage sale.

SPIDER SPOON AND SKIMMER

I love my large spider spoon, used to move food into or out of hot liquids. It is useful for noodles, blanching vegetables, and gracefully adding some deep-roasted vegetables to an otherwise finished pot of soup.

A small fine-mesh skimmer also comes in handy when making jams and compotes, doing any serious frying, or straining components of a salad dressing.

STAND MIXER AND FOOD PROCESSOR

Expensive new, but both stand mixers and food processors are obtainable for much less, in perfect working order, through diligent searching.

I am happy to have initially learned to cook from my mother who never uses any tools whatsoever, doing most everything with her hands, bowls, and knives. It gave me an appreciation for doing most of the work without help, and it's definitely possible. That said, both the food processor and stand mixer are essential players in my kitchen.

TALL-RIMMED STAINLESS STEEL SAUTÉ PAN

A basic heavy-bottomed stainless steel sauté pan with a lid gets so much action in my kitchen. The edges are tall enough that it is my preferred pan for cooking pasta (especially long noodles) quickly. It is also great for sauces and sautéed vegetables.

The Pantry

ARBORIO RICE, WILD RICE, AND SUSHI RICE

I buy bulk arborio rice and keep it in a hermetically sealed jar, ready at all times for a spontaneous risotto. Sometimes the international foods market will have good, vacuum-packed boxes of it on sale, which will be of equal or higher quality, and perhaps a better value.

As a native Oregonian, I have a strong taste for wild rice. My mother would make it as an accompaniment to fish and meat dishes during my childhood. I learned to cook it before I ever learned to cook brown rice. I keep some wild rice around always, and most often use it in improvised suppers, where it usually makes the meal.

I keep sushi rice around also, and always prepare it in a rice cooker, after five or six washings. Two friends once worked on a rice farm in Japan, and they returned insisting on washing rice until the water runs clear, then when the rice is done, dressing it with mirin and rice vinegar, while stirring to let the steam out.

ASIAN SAUCES AND SEASONINGS

- Fish sauce (one bottle of the standard, thin, cheap "tea" consistency kind, and another of the slightly syrupy, rounder-flavored, fancier kind)
- Oyster sauce (a thick, sweet soy sauce with a funky deliciousness, amazing on brassicas)
- Tamari (classic, best-flavored soy sauce)
- Ponzu (citrus soy sauce; so bright, so good)
- Kombu ponzu (if you can find it; this rounder-flavored ponzu made with sea vegetables is my favorite)
- Mirin (sweet rice wine, to achieve balance with all the salty soy)
- Wasabi oil (get a tiny, tiny bottle, and dribble it once or twice on top of hot soups; the fumes will clear your nasal passages before you even take a bite)
- Bonito flakes (for making dashi and adding to smoking hot anything)
- Wakame and kombu (dried seaweed, in flakes or strips, from the Japanese grocery)

BLACK PEPPER

For years I didn't have a nice pepper grinder. They are expensive, and it didn't feel like a priority. When I was a kid at the neighborhood Italian restaurant, I found the 15-inch-tall pepper grinder looming over my salad, wielded almost threateningly by the waiter, to be absurd and mildly terrifying. Maybe that's why I didn't see it as a priority.

Then I found a beautiful, compact, made-in-the-USA wooden pepper grinder at a thrift store for four dollars. Five years later, I found another. Now one lives in the dining area, the other in the kitchen. I couldn't live without them. I recommend splurging on a new one, or really doing the work to find a deal on a nice used one.

BOTTLED LEMON JUICE AND FRESH LEMONS

I traveled in Turkey a few years ago. On the first day in Istanbul we were wandering around with our rucksacks weighing down our shoulders, fresh from a stretch in France, Germany, Poland, and Hungary, where the food was delicious but entirely without "zing." We found a welcoming café and ordered large bowls of salad. They had bottles of lemon juice and olive oil on the table. I remember just dousing my cucumbers and greens with the lemon juice bottle, loving the unusual taste (mellower, having been in a bottle, and with lemon oil to help preserve it) and zing zing zing. I ate a balik ekmek, the Turkish fish sandwich (see my recipe, page 88), every day after that. What was commonly set out for customers? The bottled lemon juice.

Returning home, I sought out something higher quality than the neon yellow bottles I associated with college alcoholics' dorm room drinking supplies, and found Nellie & Joe's Key West Lemon Juice. The taste is exquisite, the company genuine, and nothing weird is added. It tastes like its Turkish sister. I keep a bottle in the fridge always, for acidulating water to soak vegetables, for making salad dressing, for marinades, for dousing over fish, for tossing into a pan for a final flavor lift, and so on.

That said, I also love working with fresh lemons, and am rarely without them in the kitchen. My family friend, Sheila, who was an early inspiration for the way I cook and eat, sends me a box from her yard in California every year. If you have any connections in California or Florida, try to work it.

BREAD

There is no point in ever consuming bad or even "regular" bread if very good bread is available to you or within your means to bake at home. The extra dollar or two, the trip to the bakery, the hours of work, whatever it is, is worth it.

DRIED SPICES

We've all probably had a spice rack, spice bag, or spice drawer that is over-stuffed with stale spices. Figure out what spices you actually use frequently, and keep a manageable amount of them in sealable jars.

- Dried herbs: basil, oregano, thyme (from the home garden)
- Paprika: only get good old-school Hungarian paprika, sweet and hot
- Powders: cardamom, cinnamon, cumin, garam masala, garlic, ginger, green garlic, mustard, onion, turmeric, white pepper
- Seeds: caraway, cumin, coriander, fennel, fenugreek, mustard
- Spice blends: gomashio, za'atar
- Other: cardamom pods, star anise, whole nutmeg

DRIED WILD MUSHROOMS

I buy dried wild mushrooms from a small stand at the farmers' market, when their abundance keeps the prices down, then store them in tall jars.

Having ready access to dried porcinis has changed my Italian cooking for the better.

If you have a dehydrator (or a friend with one), I recommend foraging and dehydrating them yourself!

FANCY VINEGARS

A kitchen skill I was never taught? Using acids. I learned it by using my taste buds and plenty of experimentation. The use of acid is essential to my cooking, and you'll see it come up again and again in these pages. I keep an absurd

fleet of vinegars in the cupboard: white wine, tarragon white wine, aged white wine, red wine, sherry, malt, muscatel, blood orange, umeboshi plum, rice, and a few kinds of balsamic. If looking to change your vinegar game, I recommend springing for some nice French tarragon white wine and muscatel vinegars. They will bring new life to your vegetables.

GOOD BUTTER

I buy butter from a market that sells to restaurants and bakeries and magically carries one pound blocks of local butter at a lower price, perhaps because it hasn't been cut into four sticks and isn't in a box. I enjoy splurging sometimes on fancy European butter. Italian buffalo butter is a real treat; New Zealand butter tends to taste of grass, in a good way. French butter, reminiscent of cheese, sprinkled with salt, is worth every penny. Making or buying cultured butter is also recommended, if it is something you'd like to try.

OIL

In this book, when I say "oil," use whatever oil you prefer with a mild flavor profile. I sat through one too many "what oil other than olive oil should we use?" conversations in my college co-op days, and it doesn't really matter. Maybe you like canola, or safflower, or grapeseed, or peanut, or corn oil.

When I say "olive oil," use good quality but not terribly expensive olive oil. If I say "grassy olive oil," I'm talking about a greener, spicier, finishing olive oil. My preference is grassy, though if fruity is your favorite, this is what you should use instead! I am not going to assume everyone always has a fleet of oils on hand at all times.

QUALITY DRIED PASTA

I go for the organic, all-semolina Italian stuff in the brown paper bags. Or really beautifully packaged pastas from the slightly upscale market. If you have an old-fashioned Italian deli in your area, go there; they usually have both at lower prices. In general, feel out the quality of the pasta by its packaging and how the package feels in your hands. You'll know!

SALT

I am quite loyal to English Maldon flaky sea salt for finishing or for any application where the salt plays a very important role (such as oatmeal). In this book, "salt" means kosher or other fine California sea salt and "flaky salt" means Maldon.

I do also like Celtic sea salt or sel gris, the wet, chunky, grey varieties from France.

SALT-PACKED ANCHOVIES

I prefer using the larger, salt-packed Italian anchovies from the huge tin, which I dole out into a few Weck jars after they're open. I find them to be more versatile than the oily little anchovies in a jar, though it does take a bit of work to wash, soak, and debone them before using. Once you get in the routine, it's quite enjoyable, really.

SWEETNESS

I use ginger syrup from The Ginger People, and Lyle's Golden Syrup (an English light treacle syrup) as sweetener in several recipes in this book. They are a major tool in balancing the acidity of lemon juice and vinegars in my savory cooking, and are also excellent in baking and preparing cooked fruit. I also use honey, maple syrup, and dark brown sugar. For refined sugar, it's organic evaporated cane juice and a small stash of powdered sugar.

UDON NOODLES

A sealable package with five or six rolls of udon noodles is always in my cupboard, ready for a Japanese-leaning stir-fry or noodle soup with mushrooms and greens.

Suggested Alternatives

If an ingredient is perhaps unique to the home garden, to the Pacific Northwest, or unlikely to be found anywhere without access to farms growing unusual ingredients, I've provided a suggested alternative, shown in the ingredients lists. For example, the Apricots and White Currants with Elderflower recipe on page 241 calls for white currants, as many as you like, or seedless white wine grapes or other tart fruit.

Quantities

I tend to be sparing with specific quantities and measurements for most of the recipes in this book. This is a slight nod to cookery books of old, where the writer often assumes the cooks can figure it out themselves. Unless it is essential to the success of the dish, I've left it out. I want to free you of the stilted pace created by exact measurement cooking. Use your fats and acids wisely. Learn how that ladelful of pasta water will make your whole dish come together. Learn how to build up the flavors in each dish—fry the spices, roast the garlic, deglaze the onions with the wine, burn the edges of the peppers, dress the crisp vegetables with vinegar. Make soup with confidence, knowing it will taste delicious because of how you prepared it, even if it looks like you are just throwing ingredients into a pot. Develop a personal kitchen madness and refine your own method. Consider what your taste really is. Learn how to adjust to your taste on the fly. Always try and make the food you most want to eat. If you aren't sure about what you love and what you most want to eat, go out in the world and figure it out (peruse cookbooks, eat out, call your mom) and then get back in the kitchen.

Portions

You will notice a complete absence of the common cookbook notation: "Serves _____." Every recipe will serve approximately three people, as they did during the real-time shooting of the book. Three-person (or at least, three-adult) households are perhaps uncommon, and yet with portions for approximately three, two can eat a lot or four can eat smaller portions as part of a larger meal. Halve or double these basic three-person recipes to serve only one or to serve as many as five or six. Some of the three-person recipes that are presented as salads or side dishes can be enjoyed very easily as a main course for two. Cakes and pies are designed to fit common baking vessels and will serve three or four with a day or two of leftovers. The same is true for the soups and risottos.

Preheating

In most cases I won't note a preheating temperature since the majority of cookbooks instruct you to flip on the oven ages before it's necessary. Simply look toward the end of the recipe and find "Bake at _____ degrees F for _____ minutes" and preheat the oven when you're ready.

Seasonality: From Winter to Fall, and All Over Again

Each chapter (Soups, Salads, Sandwiches, and so on) is organized seasonally, from winter to fall. In the first chapter, we begin with a soup featuring all the winter vegetables and end with a hot borscht for when the cold has decidedly arrived again.

At the end of some chapters, there are sets of seasonal variations on a dish, marked Seasonal Staples, also organized from winter to fall. These are some of my favorite, frequently made dishes.

TASTES, COLORS, AND TEXTURES OF THE SEASONS

Winter: Hearty soups with vinegary steam rising and clearing the senses; crusty walnut bread; watching the sun come up over the hill; seeing the hoar-frost on the plants out front; eating spiced porridge; sipping hot, bright coffee. Potatoes in every preparation, salty and briny shellfish, dark ribbons of kale, and sage brown-butter added to everything.

Spring: Plates of delicately cultivated, vivid greens and purples from the garden, from tiny lettuces to tight stalks of asparagus. Also foraged wild foods, from nettles and morels to fiddleheads and ramps. Chalky white sheep's cheeses, streaky pink rhubarb, and whole fish baked in parchment with aromatic leaves.

Summer: Scalding, juicy, succulent eggplant; sweet, lip-smacking tomatoes; young mild garlic added to everything. The crunch of cucumbers and that green bean you eat raw, just to test it. The smell of freshly picked herbs on your hands as you move from slicing to dicing and back again, working through the abundance. The bursting berries, tart at first and progressively sweeter, then at last the dripping figs and first tart apples.

Fall: The strong herbaceous bite of good celery, eaten fresh and also cooked in butter. The earthy scent of mushrooms cooking in heavy pans, of squash and carrots and onions and potatoes roasting while the rain falls against the kitchen window. Floral, bright apples with names you can never remember and skin you can never photograph well enough. Syrupy pears and crumbling sharp cheeses, golden ales, and rye bread.

SOUPS

soup for Sibylle Baier

One weekend while visiting my hometown in the depths of winter, I was to make supper for our small family. With only myself and my parents to feed and the feelings of nostalgia and comfort abounding, I settled on picking up one of each winter vegetable and then improvising. As the frost filled the windows, I worked to the soundtrack of a folk album that had been recorded in the seventies but was recently discovered and released for the first time—*Colour Green* by Sibylle Baier.

I found the album a year or two before, but had my most poignant listen just a few months earlier while traveling in the back of a small van through Germany. I could easily recall looking out at the brittle trees disappearing in the fog of the ancient forests as Sibylle sang of losing something in the hills. I couldn't imagine a more appropriate setting to really absorb the album. Though I was back in Oregon, it was still winter. The album still sounded just as good.

Lots of butter

1 yellow onion

1 shallot

1 leek

½ large or 1 whole small celeriac (celery root)

Dijon mustard

1 turnip

1 rutabaga (swede)

Salt

3 Yukon Gold potatoes

Alcohol of some kind (white wine, dry vermouth, fine beer, or whiskey)

Pickle juice(s)

Apple cider vinegar

1 small scoop of sauerkraut

1 bulb garlic

Bouillon of some kind

Lemon pepper (This is here because it was in my mom's spice cabinet when I first made the soup, from a spice-blend maker in Eugene. You can make your own with dried lemon zest and cracked black pepper, or just approximate with whatever you like.)

Good crusty bread (rye, whole wheat, or sourdough)

1 medium paper bag filled with cultivated mushrooms (cremini or white button)

(*Continued*)

In a large soup pot, melt an entire stick of butter over medium heat as you chop the alliums: the onion, roughly lengthwise; the shallot, medium dice; the leek, ½-inch circles (white part), reserving the green tops.

Drop the onion and shallot in as soon as the melted butter covers the bottom of the stockpot. Shake and cover. Slice the celeriac into short cigarette-size pieces. Add them to the pot. Shake. Add a generous plop of Dijon mustard. The aromatics of the mustard will immediately be released and infuse the rest of the food—cover swiftly to trap them. Cook for approximately 5 minutes, stirring three or four times to ensure that everything cooks evenly. Halfway through, add the leeks. Shake. While this operation is happening, chop the turnip and the rutabaga into large yet thin-ish pieces. Put them in a large mixing bowl filled with water. Shake salt in and mix it around with your hand. The water will draw out of some of bitter flavors and soften the fibers of the vegetables. Chop the potatoes.

When it looks like the alliums and celeriac are translucent and delicious, turn the heat up to high and remove the lid. They will start to sizzle and brown a bit. At the right moment, push the food aside and find the spots browning on the bottom of the pot. Deglaze the pot with your alcohol of choice, vigorously scraping with the wooden spoon to release the browned, extra-flavorful bits.

Return to medium heat. Add a hefty splash of pickle juice, preferably from a few kinds of pickles. Add a dash of apple cider vinegar as well. Then add the potatoes and sauerkraut, and cover again.

Around this time, prep the garlic bulb for roasting. Take a knife and slice off the tops of the cloves, keeping the bulb whole, then pull off the most papery skin. Get out a baking dish. Melt ½ stick butter. Sprinkle the top of the garlic generously with salt, then pour some butter over it. Tear the green leek tops with your hands, splitting them at the top and pulling so they come apart. You can also slice them thinly in long strips. Toss with the remaining butter. Salt and pepper them. Bake at 350 degrees F until the leek tops are crisp and charred in a few places and garlic is softened. (This is a slightly different method for the same soup topping as on page 33.) The leeks should be done before the garlic.

Prepare a tasty broth in a mixing bowl using the bouillon mixed with warm water (approximately 4 cups) or prepared stock. Taste it and add powdered garlic, onions, whatever might make it taste good on its own. Add the broth along with the drained turnips and rutabaga to the pot. Stir well. Add lemon pepper (or your own approximation). Cover and turn the heat up to high until it starts to boil. Stir actively, and reduce the heat to low.

Let the soup simmer for 1 hour. Keep an eye on the roasting garlic and leeks. You want them to brown lightly and crisp. Moving them around in the dish will help. Also heat up crusty bread of some kind—dark rye is my favorite with this soup.

I had sent a different soup recipe to Asher earlier that season and he had just requested another, so I took care to jot down notes as I cooked the soup. He'd been with me on the ride through the German hills and he knew Sibylle's album, so I figured he'd really "get" this soup. I remember taking a moment to send him the recipe while letting the soup simmer on the stove, before calling my parents to the table. Asher went on to make it several times for groups of friends on the East Coast, and both of us have continued to pass it along to others.

About 15 minutes before you intend to eat, slice the mushrooms and sauté them in butter (best in a cast-iron) until crisped up and chestnut brown. Don't crowd the mushrooms! You might need to do three pans' worth for each batch to have enough space. As you finish each batch, drop them into the soup and cover again. If there is pan residue, deglaze again with alcohol and tip into the soup.

When all is ready, do a final stir-up, season to taste (really, you shouldn't need to salt or anything, but maybe a splash of apple cider vinegar will make it perfect). Make a fine paste from the roasted garlic. Stir a spot of roasted garlic paste into each bowl of the soup right before serving. Top with the crispy leeks and serve with the bread and more butter.

down east chowdah

I made this soup for the first time on the last night of a summer trip to Maine. I'd been staying with Asher and his girlfriend Marit, whose folks own this beautiful "camp" (a common term for a modest house, uninhabitable in the winter but used every summer) out in Perry—almost as Down East as you can get.

Marit had been making great, simple sourdough the whole week and left us some fully formed loaves to bake while she went to a milk-bottling shift at a nearby seventh-generation farm. Before she left, she called up all the places in the area where one might buy fish and talked to them in her best Mainer accent: "Howsa catch today, Patti?" Then said, still affecting the accent, "Boys, go get you some fish and make us some chowdah. I'll be back when all that milk is bottled."

Luckily, we had some of that exquisite raw milk to work with, some already-boiled potatoes, so much parsley, a few lemons, and a lot of butter. We jumped in the Volvo and drove to the fish market. We chose one pound of clams and one pound of haddock. "Just pulled this here seafood in two hours ago, boys," said the lady.

We cranked the oven up and threw the bread in, opened some wine, then started making the chowder, improvisation-style. The milk bottling took longer than planned, and the torturous waiting really added to the triumphant chow down.

We ate it so hungrily and happily, I flew home thinking about it the whole way. A few days later, I made the chowder again and wrote it down.

Several potatoes, either fingerling or Yukon Gold (the point is waxy but forgiving)

Salt

½ cup (1 stick) butter

1 onion

White wine

½ bulb of garlic (optional)

1 pound clams

Additional fancy fish if you can afford it or if someone else is buying (crab, lobster, or even fresh mussels)

Milk

1 bunch parsley

1 pound rockfish, cod, or other seasonal, affordable white fish

1 lemon

Crusty bread

An extra clove of garlic and butter for the bread

Get a pot of water boiling for the potatoes. Depending on their size, slice them in half or in quarters. Salt the water generously. Proceed with the next few steps of the recipe, dropping in the potatoes when the water boils.

Melt the butter in a large soup pot over medium heat. Dice the onion (don't be too concerned about uniformity) and drop it in. Stir and let the onion soften in the butter, sprinkling a little salt over it. While bubbles form around the onion pieces, add a healthy splash of wine and stir. Peel and chop the garlic and drop it in when the onions are translucent. Continue cooking over medium-low, stirring regularly with a wooden spoon. When the onions and garlic have lightly colored and completely softened with the wine and butter, turn the heat off.

(Continued)

When the potatoes give to a fork but don't crumble, remove them from the water with a spider spoon or pour the pot out over a colander with a bowl below to collect the potato water and return it to the pot. Keep it warm over low heat.

Wash and scrub the clams to ensure that all the sand is removed. Add them to a small saucepan with a ladleful of potato water and a splash of wine. Turn the heat up to medium-high, cover partially, and let alone for a few minutes then start checking frequently. When the clams have begun opening up, turn off the heat and cover completely. After a minute or two, take the lid off and discard any clams that haven't opened. Take out the good clams and pour your perfect clam jus to the soup pot.

Remove the clams from their shells. I like to use scissors to snip off the little black "tongues," but it's not necessary—just for aesthetics! Rinse the shells one more time and then put them in the potato water.

If you are using crab, lobster, or mussels, prepare the meat. After removing from the shells, set the meat aside.

Chop the cooked potatoes then add them to the soup pot. The heat should still be off. Pour in enough milk to reach about halfway up the pot. Add a cup of the potato-clamshell water. Stir, taste, stir, and add more liquid (of either kind) to reach your desired consistency. Add the clams and the fancy shellfish.

De-stem and chop the parsley. Carefully slice your fish into long bite-size pieces.

Turn the heat on under the soup pot. When you hold your hand over it and feel the broth radiating some heat, add the fish. Set a timer for 3 minutes. Watch closely. The liquid should start to bubble. When you see the first bubbles (the beginning of a boil), turn off the heat whether the 3 minutes is up or not. Stir in the parsley. The fish will cook in the hot liquid, and the decreasing heat should keep it from overcooking.

One can eat the soup when the fish is opaque and done, but it's best when you've lidded and taken it off the heat, let the pot hang out for 30 to 60 minutes, then slowly reheated it on low. Add a squeeze of lemon juice to each serving.

Eat this with hot, crusty bread rubbed with garlic and slathered in butter.

Leftovers:

Part of the experience of making this chowder is saving enough to have for breakfast the next day. The first time it was on the first very cold morning at the end of summer—the first sign of fall. We brought the hot soup outside and opened the aluminum foil bundle of garlic bread to let the stream billow into the cold air. We chased the hot nourishing soup with smoky cups of coffee.

buttermilk potato/leek soup, with kohlrabi

Out of nowhere, an old friend asked for "that amazing potato-leek soup recipe." I didn't know what he was talking about, but I love potato-leek soup, and it was winter. So this was my attempt at coming up with something worthy of such a status. I thought about some of the meal scenes in Chekhov short stories, where travelers come in from the cold and eat with hunched shoulders these restorative, humble meals.

5 medium Yukon Gold potatoes	2 cups buttermilk, plus more to taste
1 large russet potato	Good sour cream
Salt	White pepper
¼ cup (½ stick) butter	Duck fat (optional)
Mild oil	Black pepper
3 leeks	Crispy Leek Tops (recipe follows)
1 onion	Sunchoke Chips (recipe follows)
3 green kohlrabi	Very good bread
¼ cup heavy cream or half-and-half	Butter

(Continued)

Fill a medium soup pot halfway with water. Turn the burner to high, then swiftly peel all the Yukon Gold potatoes, adding each one to the water as you finish peeling it. Peel and chop the russet in half and drop it in the pot. Reserve the potato peels. Let the water reach a boil then reduce to a simmer, with a healthy shaking of salt.

In another soup pot or a big saucepan, melt the butter with a glug of oil around it. Slice the leeks, up to the light-green part, into ¼-inch medallions. Wash in a small bowl then add to the pot. Peel the onion, cut in half, slice into ¼-inch curves, add to the pot, and cover. You want the alliums to sweat and go translucent.

Trim the kohlrabi and slice into ¼-inch rounds. Stack them four pieces tall and cut into triangular quarters. Take the onion skins, potato peelings, kohlrabi trimmings, and any other good vegetable trimmings you have around and set them aside, ready to become stock.

When the potatoes are tender, remove them with tongs or a spider spoon. Return the water to a rolling boil and add the kohlrabi pieces, setting a timer for 3 minutes. Prepare a cold-water bath for the kohlrabi. When the 3 minutes are up, move the kohlrabi to the cold water and add the vegetable scraps to the hot water. Continue cooking on high until the stock begins to darken a little in color, then reduce to a simmer.

Chop half of the cooked potatoes into smaller pieces, leaving the other half whole for the moment. If you have a potato ricer, load it with the chopped pieces of potato and rice into the soup pot over the leeks and onions. Repeat as many times as needed. If you don't have a ricer, it's okay; this is just a trick to get the consistency extra smooth. A similar effect can be achieved with a potato masher or an enthusiastic fork.

Stir everything with a wooden spoon, adding salt and white pepper. Pour in the cream. Then, using an immersion blender, lightly blend the potatoes, onions, and leeks. You can let everything hang out at this stage if the veggie stock isn't ready yet, and focus on another element of your meal. When the veggie stock is ready, get rid of the scraps by passing the stock through a fine-mesh sieve. Pour a couple ladlefuls into the mixture, blend until you have a very smooth puree, and taste it. It should be like your favorite "normal" potato leek soup! Maybe it needs more salt or white pepper? Add as you see fit.

Slice the remaining whole potatoes into bite-size pieces that roughly match the kohlrabi pieces. Add them all to the soup, along with two or three more ladlefuls of stock. Right here, it should be just slightly too thick, but almost the right consistency. Add the buttermilk, stir in, and warm on medium-low until heated through but not really bubbling away. Taste now, with a bite of kohlrabi. If it isn't quite tangy enough, add more buttermilk. At this point, I often exercise my lenient pescatarianism and add a big knob of duck fat.

When everything is ready, ladle the soup into bowls. Top with one spoonful of sour cream (to stir in for a final luscious "lift"), crack a bunch of black pepper into one corner, throw on some Crispy Leek Tops and Sunchoke Chips. Eat with bread and butter.

CRISPY LEEK TOPS

The green, usually unwanted, tops of leeks
Melted butter, olive oil, or duck fat
Fine salt

Cut the leek tops into thin strips with a good knife, or tear them with your hands. Arrange on a baking dish and toss with melted butter, olive oil, or duck fat. Season with a little bit of fine salt.

Depending on the quantity of leek tops and where they are going (on top of a soup, tossed with pasta, or in a quiche), either broil them or bake them at 350 degrees F. With broiling, it all happens very quickly and you'll end up with more

(Continued)

papery-crisp charred ends. With baking, it takes about 10 to
15 minutes, and requires that you take the pan out and shift the
pieces around. The end result is a little greener and the flavor
more concentrated, though it is slightly more difficult to arrive
at the desired crispiness.

SUNCHOKE CHIPS

Sunchokes (3 or 4 usually provide plenty of chips)

Oil

Fine salt

Slice the sunchokes as thinly as you can without them being
that "shaved" consistency—that's too thin.

Lay them on a baking sheet, separated from each other like
cookies. You can do this on baking parchment if you want
to be extra careful to avoid burning them, however they will
be slower to crisp up. I've done it successfully both with and
without parchment.

Pour a little oil into a small dish or cup, then use a pastry
brush to brush oil on the top side of each piece. Season with a
powdery, fine salt. It's even better if you crush some salt with a
mortar and pestle. Then meticulously turn each slice over and
repeat the process.

Bake on the center rack at 300 degrees F. After about 8 minutes, start checking them. Remove them when they've turned
golden brown and are thin and dry like chips. The pieces at the
edges of the pan (and the thinnest ones) will finish first.

Flip them over if it seems like the bottoms are getting done
but the tops have a ways to go or vice versa. Continue returning to the oven, checking and removing finished ones every
couple of minutes until they are all toasty light brown, with
a deep savory flavor. This will be a mildly annoying and
time-consuming job, but is totally worth it and this is the only
way to get it done.

nettle dumplings in sorrel broth

One year on my birthday at this perfect small restaurant with one cook, a long counter, a few tables, and a chalkboard menu, I ate dumplings like these, covered in walnut cream sauce. I had become interested in cooking with nettles for the first time that same year, and these were the best I'd ever tasted. After experimenting for a while to get them right, I came up with this cleansing, clear soup, which is perfect for a rainy night.

Turnips	Pecorino, Asiago, or Parmesan cheese
Carrots	1 egg for every 20 dumplings
Onions	Flaky salt
Oil	Black pepper
Salt	1 bunch sorrel
1 bunch parsley	Lemon
A vast quantity of nettles (they cook down like spinach, and if you're already out in the woods harvesting them you might as well go big)	

You can use any delicious broth starter such as prepared vegetable, mushroom, or chicken stock here, but if you have the time and inclination, this vegetable broth works particularly nicely for this dish. To make the broth, roast turnips, carrots, and onions tossed with a little oil and salt at 300 degrees F for 2 to 3 hours, until their flavor is extremely roasty and concentrated. You can do this a day or two in advance.

Wash the parsley well to remove any grit. Cover the roasted vegetables with water in a large soup pot, and bring to a boil. Add the parsley and reduce to a simmer for an hour or two. When the taste is right, pass through a sieve and discard the vegetables.

To make the dumplings, wearing gloves, snip the best leaves from the nettle plants, discarding the rest. When you're halfway done, bring a pot of water to a boil. Add a little salt.

Wash the nettle leaves in cold water. Add to the boiling water in batches and cook for 90 seconds. The sting will disappear and the color will brighten.

(Continued)

Remove to your largest bowl filled with cold water. Wait for the water to return to a boil, then repeat until you've blanched all the nettles, then drain the large bowl.

Grate your cheese finely.

When the nettles are all done, drained, and are cool enough to handle, set the bowl next to the sink, pick up large handfuls and squeeze them, which should release a large quantity of green liquid. Toss these squeezed balls of condensed nettles back into the bowl and repeat until they're all in this state, dumping out any residual water from the bowl as well.

Pull each ball out onto a cutting board, chopping roughly with your biggest knife. Repeat. Toss with the cheese in the large bowl. Crack an egg and beat it in a separate bowl. Add it to the nettle mixture, stirring. If it seems a little dry or separated still, beat another egg and repeat. When the consistency is right (think pretty dry cookie batter), add flaky salt and black pepper to taste.

Form this mixture into small balls with your hands. Steam in a steamer, a Chinese steam bun rack, or a colander over a pot of water. The color should dull a little bit, and the balls should form into a sturdier construction. Remove from the heat.

Right before serving, gently heat the broth until steam swirls out of the pot, then chiffonade the sorrel and add the leaves. They will dull in color but release their delicate, lemony flavor all through the broth.

Ladle the hot broth into warmed bowls (do this in the oven or by pouring hot water from a kettle and swirling it around, then draining), then add 4 or 5 dumplings to each bowl. Grate over some extra pecorino, follow with a squeeze from a wedge of lemon, and serve.

M. F. K. oyster stew

Sofie wooed me with a copy of M. F. K. Fisher's *Consider the Oyster*, with little notes and cards stuck throughout its pages. The inscription read "Let's make some of this stuff and read it out loud to each other." I knew she was being somewhat sarcastic, but secretly I really wanted to.

There are two recipes for oyster stew in the first section of the book made so simply that it's almost unbelievable. The difference is that one features celery salt and the other paprika. One cream, the other milk. They are written by others, published before M. F. K.'s book, and given due credit. The following is my interpretation of both, pared down to serve two to three and given some extra oomph.

---

1 or 2 cloves of garlic (fresh young garlic if in season)	⅓ to ½ stick butter, plus more for the pan
Tarragon white wine vinegar	1 (8- to 10-ounce) jar extra-small shucked oysters in their liquid
Celery salt	Good Hungarian paprika
1 fresh raw oyster per person	Oyster crackers
2 to 4 cups whole milk	

First make the mignonette sauce and prep the oyster shooters. Peel and mince the garlic. Place in a little dish and cover with the vinegar to macerate. Sprinkle in a little celery salt, stir, and leave alone.

Scrub the raw oyster shells well and then shuck them, doing your best to keep as much of their liquid in the shell as possible, while also checking for any sand that may have slipped in! Set on ice in a bowl in the fridge while preparing the rest of the stew.

For the stew, heat a heavy-bottomed saucepan or soup pot on medium. The original recipe has you "wipe the pan but don't clean it, so the milk won't stick." In this spirit, drop a small pat of butter in the pan, use a spatula to grease the surface, and then the milk: start with about 2 cups, or a little more if you're cooking for a crowd. I always err on the cautious side here, and set aside some to add after the oysters to balance it all out.

When the milk is heated through (though it must not boil), add the jarred oysters and their liquid. Reduce the heat to just shy of medium, and cook for about 2½ minutes, stirring often, watching the oysters closely so they

(Continued)

Having plucked a theme right out of the cold November air, my childhood friend Lucas and I are up well past midnight cooking and eating a Hungarian feast for two. We drink a large bottle of questionable homemade mead, gifted by a former roommate. This evolves clumsily into Secret Restaurant Portland, a supper club we've been doing ever since.

do not curl! Add paprika and celery salt to taste. It is at this point that you may feel compelled to add more milk, perhaps if the stew is too oystery for your taste.

After another 2½ minutes (approximately the 5 minute mark), the oysters should be cooked to perfection, the broth hot and flavorful, and all the ingredients will have had a chance to get to know one another. Add the butter and stir just a little to melt it. The butter should separate slightly and rise to the surface, which will be delectable.

Take the pan off the heat and portion the stew out into dark bowls. Add the mignonette sauce to the oysters on the half shell, then float them in the center of each bowl. Sprinkle with paprika and celery salt. Get out the oyster crackers. Take the oyster shooter, letting the curious liquor and tangy sauce trickle down your throat. Then gobble some oyster crackers. Before swallowing all of them, take your first spoonful of oyster stew. This comes about as close to manufacturing a guaranteed oyster euphoria as I can get.

If you want to get really into it, you can even use the oyster shell as your spoon. Continue eating, with plenty of crackers, and a crisp beer or white wine.

black bean soup with roasted tomatillos

I've been making this soup since my college days. My sophomore year, while doing an internship in Montréal, I lived with a Venezuelan man fourteen years my senior named Angelo. (He was the only person on Craigslist who would take me.) For one meal he made me empanadas filled with sheep's milk feta, and I made him this soup. He said it was the best he'd had since his mother's. He pinpointed the secret ingredient—ginger—which nearly no one has been able to do in the years since then.

1 pound dry black beans	Lemon or lime juice
Onions	Coriander seeds
Garlic	Cumin seeds
Ginger	Mustard seeds
6 or 7 tomatillos (this will make more sauce than you need, but the leftovers will be useful)	A couple bay leaves
	1 spicy pepper, such as jalepeño or Hungarian wax pepper
Olive oil	Cayenne (optional)
Salt	Crema (optional)
Black pepper	

This soup has a very simple construction. Soak the black beans overnight. Mince the onions, garlic, and ginger (quantities catered to your tastes) as finely as possible. This will take a while, or you can do it in the food processor. I like the labor involved in the slicing and dicing.

To make the tomatillo sauce, preheat the oven to 375 degrees F. Remove the papery skins of the tomatillos, wash them under cold water, and chop into quarters. In a roasting tin, toss the tomatillos with a little oil and salt. Prepare a bulb of garlic for roasting: slice off the top of the bulb and remove the papery skins, pour oil over the exposed cloves, and top with lots of salt. Nestle the bulb among the tomatillos. Roast for 45 minutes to 1 hour. Puree the roasted tomatillos with 2 to 5 cloves of roasted garlic. (Save the rest for another dish.) Add salt, pepper, and lemon or lime juice to taste. Set aside while the soup simmers.

Heat oil in a heavy-bottomed soup pot over medium-high heat, add generous pinches of coriander, cumin, and mustard seeds. The bottom of the soup

(Continued)

pot should be scattered with seeds. When they start to pop, add the minced onion, garlic, and ginger, then reduce the heat to medium. Salt generously and stir frequently, cooking until quite soft.

Drain the black beans and add them to the pot, covering the mixture with at least 1 inch of fresh water, then raise the heat to a boil. Tie the bay leaves and spicy pepper up in a piece of cheesecloth. When the beans are bubbling, reduce to a simmer and add the bundle.

Simmer for 1½ hours, or until the black beans are entirely tender but still hold their shape.

Salt and pepper to taste. Maybe the spicy pepper wasn't that spicy—add cayenne or lots of black pepper. Sometimes good black beans naturally have that full, round flavor. Other times they fall a little flat. What would be good here? Give it some thought with your cupboards open.

Using an immersion blender, partially blend the soup. You want a mixture of thick, pureed soup and whole bites of perfect beans.

Serve the soup with the roasted tomatillo sauce and perhaps some crema thinned with lime juice.

hearty fall stew with squash, chanterelles, and butter beans

At the first preschool where I taught, we served a lunch of beans, vegetables, grains, and fruits. My favorite lunch day was butter bean day. Slowly simmered in veggie stock, with olive oil poured on top and stirred in, I'd eat whole bowls of them. I made up this soup one day after taking a mason jar of them home with me.

---

1 smallish winter squash	Water or stock of some kind
Olive oil	1 can butter beans, rinsed and drained
Salt	2 large handfuls of chanterelle mushrooms
Black pepper	Apple cider vinegar
1 onion	Smashed walnuts
Butter	Rustic whole wheat country bread

Slice the squash in half, scoop out the seeds, and peel the outer skin with a paring knife. Then cut each side into long strips. Slice the strips into thirds, then toss with oil, salt, and pepper. Bake at 425 degrees F for 30 minutes, scraping, flipping, and agitating. Lower the heat to 375 degrees F and bake for another 30 minutes, continuing to scrape, flip, and agitate. Lower the heat to 325 degrees F and bake for another 30 minutes, continuing to scrape, flip, and agitate. Turn the oven off but leave the pan in the oven until it cools. (This time-lapse roasted squash can be used in innumerable dishes. This soup first came about using the second half of a large batch of squash I had made for something else.)

Perhaps you might roast an onion along with the squash. If not, cook the onion in butter in the soup pot as per the standard soup-making practice. Slice the onion lengthwise and cook it in olive oil until translucent and a bit browned, then add several cups of water or stock. Add half the squash, stir, and salt to taste. Then use an immersion blender to puree. Thin or thicken as desired by adding more water or squash during this process. When the consistency is correct, add the butter beans and the other half of the squash. Crack in loads of black pepper. Heat everything on low for 30 minutes or so.

Meanwhile, brush the dirt from and pull apart the chanterelle mushrooms with your fingers. Melt some butter and a few glugs of oil in a cast-iron pan. Add the mushrooms, coat, and cook on high until the moisture escapes and they are

(Continued)

swimming in buttery mushroomy juices. Heat another cast-iron skillet (preferably a thinner one—if you don't have two cast-iron pans, this second stage works in a nonstick) on high. Remove the mushrooms from the butter, adding them directly to the second dry skillet. Pour the remaining mushroomy butter into the stew. Press into the mushrooms with spatula—they will squeak. This is good.

Turn them over when they are appetizingly brown on one side. When they're done and have a perfect consistency—almost like roasted chicken, crisp edges, succulent insides—add them in great abundance to the stew. Add a little apple cider vinegar to cut through the extreme earthiness. Serve with some smashed walnuts sprinkled on top and the rustic bread.

german wild mushroom soup

My grandmother made all these soups that I assume came from her German-Midwest heritage. They were deeply savory, started with onions or leeks softened in butter, and finished with cream. I have no idea if I ever had a mushroom soup made by her, but this is an attempt at making one just the way she would have.

One November I stumbled upon a bunch of hedgehog mushrooms in a clearing, after venturing off the path during a river trail hike. My folks and I visit a cabin on the McKenzie River every fall, and the nearby woods are home to a diverse array of wild mushrooms. I wander through the trees and ferns, usually listening to 1960s folk music, with a tote bag lined in paper towels. I return to the cabin with whatever I've found around dusk, get the fire going for the evening, then improvise new dishes. This soup was one of them.

1 onion	Stock of some kind
½ bulb of garlic	Stalks of rosemary
½ cup (1 stick) butter	1 pound wild mushrooms (hedgehogs are particularly good)
1½ teaspoons Dijon mustard	2 cups heavy cream
White wine	Very good bread

Peel and quarter the onion and peel and smash the garlic. Place in a food processor and pulse carefully until it resembles a chopped, tear-inducing pile of onions and garlic (not mush!)

Melt ½ a stick of the butter in a soup pot over medium-low heat. Add the onions and garlic and stir, cover, and let sweat. When the onions and garlic have softened into a buttery mass, remove the lid and raise the heat a bit. Drop in the mustard, stir, and cover again to trap the aromatics and infuse the onions and garlic. Cook this way for a minute or so, remove the lid, and raise the heat again. When the onions and garlic are just starting to brown, push them aside and create a circle at the center of the pot. Add the wine and agitate, scraping the browned bits from the bottom, then add your stock. Wrap the stalks of rosemary in cheesecloth and add to the pot. Bring to a boil and reduce the heat to a simmer.

(Continued)

Trim and brush your mushrooms clean. Pull apart into pieces if they are quite large. In a cast-iron pan, melt the remaining ½ stick butter and sauté the mushrooms until just golden. This can be done in small batches if needed.

As the mushrooms finish, tip each batch into the soup. Once all are added, let the soup simmer on low for 30 to 60 minutes.

When it tastes awesome, discard the rosemary bundle and remove a ladle or two of mushrooms. Blend the soup partially with an immersion blender, then add back the reserved mushrooms.

Add the cream, increase the heat slowly until it has had a chance to bubble on medium-high for a moment or two, then ladle the soup into bowls. Smash a small stalk of rosemary with the blunt side of a heavy kitchen knife, then tuck it into each bowl for a last-minute herbaceous lift (removing it before tucking in yourself). Eat with some warm, crusty bread.

hot borscht, first night in Berlin style

I once rode in a freezing, unheated Eurovan from Paris to Berlin over the course of one long drizzly winter day. When Asher and I arrived in Berlin, we ascended the stairs of a crumbling apartment building to find a beautiful high-ceilinged apartment. It had wide-beamed floors and archways between the rooms, and the place was deep in preparations for a party. On the stove were hot borscht and glühwein (German mulled wine). In the oven, crusty bread. On the table, stollen (German Christmas bread) and sweet butter.

Our host, Jess, a professional dancer and choreographer who divides his time between Berlin and San Francisco, made us a quick cup of coffee to get us ready to stay up late. Sitting in that warm open kitchen and moving through the smorgasbord of borscht, bread, coffee, glühwein, stollen, and butter, made me feel more connected to my German heritage than ever before.

I asked Jess where the borscht recipe came from. He said, "It's the *Moosewood Cookbook* recipe with twenty years of experimentation and simplification." I took this as inspiration to try my own version later that winter after I was home. I made the soup again and again until I matched the taste memory of that night in Berlin.

½ head red cabbage	Caraway seeds
Red wine vinegar	Hungarian paprika
Salt	Cayenne pepper
3 large beets	Old Bay
Oil	Apple cider vinegar
Black pepper	Créme fraîche or sour cream
1 onion	Very good bread
½ bulb of garlic	

Discard the outer leaves of the cabbage if they aren't in good shape. Wash the cabbage under running water, then chop or shred it into thin pieces. Add to a large bowl and fill up with more water. Add a splash of red wine vinegar and some salt to the water—this will help take off some of the bitterness.

(Continued)

Using your best peeler, peel the beets (standing over the sink helps you not stain yourself and everything in sight). Chop the peeled beets into bite-size pieces. In a roasting tin, toss the beets with oil, salt, pepper, and red wine vinegar. Roast the beets at 400 degrees F for 25 to 40 minutes. Check and move the pieces around in the pan after about 20 minutes. You want the flavors to concentrate and some moisture to leave the beets, but you don't want them to actually dry out, caramelize, or burn.

Roughly chop the onion and garlic. (This is peasant soup; it doesn't need to be precise and doing fine little bits here is a waste of time.) Glug some oil in the bottom of a soup pot. Add the onion and garlic and cook over medium heat until they're softened and fragrant. Add a generous toss of caraway seeds and cook until you can smell them toasting.

Drain the cabbage and add it to the soup pot. Continue cooking over medium heat until the cabbage softens. Salt and pepper here, generously. When the beets are done, scrape them from the roasting tin into the soup pot. Shake in a bunch of paprika, a little cayenne, and some Old Bay or a spice with equivalent depth. When everything is soft and the colors are extra bright, throw in some more salt, then fill up the pot with water, covering the vegetables by about an inch. Bring to a boil, then reduce to a low simmer.

Add some apple cider vinegar and some more red wine vinegar to taste. You can also adjust the paprika, salt, and pepper here. The soup will be best after it has hung out on the stove, in this simmering stage, for at least an hour. Arguably, it's even better if you have one small bowl then and save the rest to serve the next day.

Eat it with dollops of créme fraîche or sour cream and good, chewy ancient grain, whole wheat, or rye bread.

SNAPSHOTS OF EATING AND COOKING

My grandmother's apartment. It is opening night for my dad's play, so it's just us. I am nine or ten years old. I sit at the table next to the kitchen while she is cooking me an intricate, very old-fashioned meal from scratch. After serving us, she resumes a game of solitaire. As I eat, pausing my run-on narrative, I can taste our family history.

SALADS

black radish, with walnuts and herbs

Black radishes: seek them out. For centuries everyone in Europe seems to have been eating them, and we're just waking up to their glories. This salad is as simple as its ingredients: black radishes, walnuts, parsley, and mint. I first came up with the idea for this salad while in Turkey, having remembered late in the day that I'd been invited to a potluck and was expected to bring something. I swung through the market street with very few lire and an appetite for something crunchy, bright, and satisfying.

½ large black radish per person

Salt

Lemon juice

1 bunch flat-leaf parsley

1 to 2 handfuls raw walnuts

1 bunch (or "healthy gathering") mint

Walnut oil

Apple cider vinegar

Honey

Shave or thinly slice the radishes. Uniformity doesn't really matter, but if you have a mandolin you aren't scared of, go ahead.

Prepare a large bowl of saltwater and lemon juice and drop slices in as you go—this will prevent the radishes from browning and will lightly pickle them, softening their burn and accentuating their tastiness.

When the radishes are all sliced and soaking, pull the parsley from its stems and chop it up. Be generous. Use more than what feels right. Meanwhile, toast the walnuts in a dry cast-iron over medium heat. Remove the walnuts when they are just starting to color and scent the air. Set them aside to cool.

Chop the mint and set it aside with the parsley.

Drain the radishes and return to the bowl. Toss with walnut oil and more lemon juice. Add apple cider vinegar to taste, and then add honey to balance. Add more salt if needed. When the radishes have had a moment to stand, dressed, and get used to their dressing, add the herbs.

Put the walnuts in a small plastic produce bag, tie it up and throw it on the floor. Stomp on it with your feet or bash it with a hammer. Open the bag and toss thoroughly with the rest of the salad.

Note: Don't be tempted to add any cheese! It will be funky and not good. Go for the crisp, refreshing crunch as a contrast to the rest of the meal.

endive, celeriac, fennel with pear and chestnuts

This is an extraordinarily balanced salad, best on days when the windows frost over and you've put on wool socks. It goes perfectly with a savory pie or bread pudding.

---

1 celeriac (celery root)	Walnut or olive oil
2 lemons (or 1 Meyer lemon, if available)	White wine vinegar (optional)
1 fennel bulb, some fronds reserved	Flaky sea salt
1 roasting tin's worth of chestnuts	1 pear (Comice, perhaps)
1 small head frisée	Crumbly cheese (aged white English-style cheddar, "coastal cheddar" recommended)

Peel the celeriac and rub all over with a halved lemon. Prepare a large bowl with water and the juice of half a lemon. Drop the celeriac in and leave it for a while.

Take it out, slice it into discs about ¼ inch thick, putting each disc back in the lemon bath as you work. Then, when you have six or seven, take out one disc at a time and julienne into matchsticks. Continue to replace in the lemon bath as you slice and julienne.

Trim the fennel and slice it as thinly as you can, dropping the slices into the lemon bath as you go.

Cut a cross into the plump side of each chestnut's skin with a paring knife. Either roast for 15 minutes at 400 degrees F or, if you have a gas range, cook in a dry cast-iron pan. When cool enough to handle (but not all the way cool, they stiffen up after leaving the sweet spot), peel, then roughly chop or pull the chestnuts apart with your hands.

Rinse, dry, and separate the frisée leaves.

In a large bowl, add the zest and juice of the remaining lemon. Add walnut oil (and maybe a drop of water or white wine vinegar here) and whisk to emulsify.

Add the frisée and drained celeriac and fennel. Dress. Toss in the chestnuts. (The salad can be held for a bit at this stage.) If the dressing is too light, add some extra oil. It may then require a dash of flaky salt or another squeeze of lemon or a splash of wine vinegar to brighten it up.

Just before serving, slice the pear and crumbly cheese, and add them both.

Divide the salad among plates and top each serving with extra fennel fronds.

lettuce, radishes, agretti, boquérones

This recipe is a very simple pairing of two common and two less-common ingredients, all used at their peak. Agretti is an Italian succulent grown for its crisp texture and tangy flavor. It can be found at farmers' markets in late spring and early summer, or grown in your garden. It can be approximated with sea beans (farmers' market or wild foraged) or something simple, like chives dressed with lemon juice. Boquérones are pickled fresh anchovies, usually from Spain or Turkey. Look for them at a fish counter or deli area of a grocery store, near the olives and pickled peppers. The basic concept and construction of this salad can be applied to other ingredients with equal success because it's a four-part system where each piece is played harmoniously. The lettuce is cool and crisp, the radishes crunchy and delicate, the agretti (or equivalent) is sour and toothsome, the boquérones are fatty, tangy, and balanced. Try it in the fall with lacinato kale (cool and crisp), kohlrabi (crunchy and delicate), thin strips of sorrel or radicchio (sour and toothsome), and torn salt-packed anchovies or salty cured pork (fatty, tangy, and balanced). This sort of remix is infinitely possible with dishes in this book, but more importantly, you can do it with any dish, anywhere, in your mind!

Lettuce, chosen for texture, color, and mild delicate flavor	Radishes (small, extra-firm ones are best)
Lemon juice	Agretti, sea beans, or some kind of sprouts, or thin strips of another crisp vegetable
Olive oil	Boquérones
Flaky sea salt	Black pepper

Wash and thoroughly dry your lettuce leaves. Dress them with lemon juice, olive oil, and a pinch of your best sea salt. Let them rest and brighten up for a few moments.

Slice the radishes super thin, sprinkling salt over them as you go. Chop the agretti into bite-size pieces, then toss with the lettuce leaves. Scatter with the radishes and toss gently to incorporate.

Lay the boquérones on last. Crack over some black pepper and serve.

watermelon radish / watercress

This is a striking, boldly flavored spring salad, with the best dressing around. The bits of lemon peel in this dressing add a floral, electric quality to anything you dress with it.

Almonds or pine nuts	1 or 2 living watercress bunches
Watermelon radishes	Meyer Lemon–Tarragon Wine Vinaigrette (recipe follows)
Salt	

Toast the almonds (you can chop them first) or pine nuts in a dry cast-iron skillet over medium heat for about 3 minutes, until just fragrant.

Slice the watermelon radishes as thinly as you can, then spread them out on a plate and sprinkle with salt to tease out the moisture a bit. Snip the leaves and tender stems off the watercress bunches with a pair of scissors. Wash them if the greens need it, but skip it if you can; watercress doesn't take being pounded with water and spun as well as other greens.

Pour off the liquid from the radishes, then combine them with the watercress leaves and dress with the Meyer Lemon–Tarragon Wine Vinaigrette. Sprinkle with the almonds or pine nuts.

MEYER LEMON–TARRAGON WINE VINAIGRETTE

1 small shallot

Salt

2 teaspoons tarragon white wine vinegar (buy the fancy French stuff or make your own—it's worth the expense or effort, seriously)

1 Meyer lemon

2 tablespoons extra-virgin olive oil

Black pepper

Peel and slice the shallot. Dice the slices finely and move them to a small bowl. Sprinkle with a pinch of salt. Add the tarragon white wine vinegar. Make sure there is enough to cover the shallot; if there isn't, add a splash more.

Juice the lemon into another small bowl. Scrape out the remnants of flesh, then, using a sharp paring knife, cut the peel into long thin strips. Add them to the shallots and vinegar. After about 10 minutes, add 1 tablespoon of olive oil to the mixture and stir again. Wait 30 minutes or so for the ingredients to break down a little and get to know one another. Then add the remaining tablespoon olive oil and all of the lemon juice. Whisk together with a fork. The dressing should be slightly creamy. Taste, adding another teaspoon of olive oil to balance the acidity if necessary. Crack in some black pepper for bite.

Before dressing your salad, dip a piece of whatever you're dressing in the bowl and taste it in action. Sometimes with a sweet vegetable, I want a bigger zing so I add more vinegar at the end. Sometimes with chicories, I want to pull it in a mellower and fattier direction and will add more olive oil (or even walnut oil).

asparagus, fava beans, pea shoots, and pecorino fresco with pesto dressing

This spring, make this salad for yourself. Do it in a fun sequence. For example, get a bundle of asparagus, and cook about half of it for dinner some night earlier in the week. Save the other half in a jar with shallow water. For that dinner, or maybe another (or some lunch), make a delicious pesto. Save a small jar of it. One of these days, use part of a lemon. Plant too many peas, so you can enjoy some of them as pea shoots. Or buy a bag from the farmers' market or thoughtful grocer. Find the best cheese counter in the place where you live, and ask them for pecorino fresco. It really must be this soft, buttery, falling apart young pecorino. If they don't have it, see if it can be brought in for you. This cheese is too delicate to handle hanging out in the fridge too long, so the day you get the cheese should be the day of the salad. Squeeze a quarter of the lemon into the leftover pesto, crack in more pepper, and, depending on the thickness of the pesto, a teaspoon or tablespoon of water, then proceed with the recipe as written.

Creamy Pesto Sauce (page 117) or your own favorite pesto

Young fava beans

½ bunch asparagus

Lemon juice

Olive oil

Salt

Black pepper

Pea shoots

Pecorino fresco

If you are starting with pesto leftover from a pasta/crostini kind of application, thin it out with a little lemon juice or water. If you are making it for this salad, just make sure the consistency is a little thinner and the taste a little tangier than you might otherwise do.

Peel the outer shells off the fava beans and drop the beans into boiling salted water. Cook for about 3 minutes, then remove to an ice bath to stop them from cooking. With a slotted spoon, remove the beans to another bowl. Peel the second shell from the favas, leaving two bright green halves.

Return the favas to the boiling water for another minute. Replenish the ice in the ice bath, then let the beans pay another visit to it. When the favas have completely cooled, remove and set aside.

Trim the woody bottom stems from the asparagus, then blanch them in the boiling water for 90 seconds, then remove to the ice bath. When completely cool, slice the stalks in half and then into bite-size strips. Dress with lemon juice, a little olive oil, salt, and pepper.

Tear the pea shoots into small pieces, just the right size for your fork, then dress with a fair amount of lemon juice. Squeeze the dressed pea shoots with your hands to tenderize them just slightly, as you might do for a raw kale salad. Follow with olive oil, salt, and pepper. Combine the pea shoots and pesto.

For each serving, portion out the dressed pea shoots and asparagus, then add the fava beans and pieces of pecorino fresco.

purple asparagus, lemon, ricotta salata

One warm, early spring I'd had my fill of the usual asparagus preparations—grilled asparagus, asparagus baked into tarts, asparagus sautéed in butter—and it was only mid-April. I bought a bunch of purple asparagus at the Saturday farmers' market and decided to only use it for salads, wanting to retain the color and try it in new ways. The candied lemon peel had been made for a batch of biscotti, I think. Ricotta salata is a frequent, always-sensible impulse buy. This salad showcases the best qualities of asparagus with simple but bold accenting flavors and textures.

1 lemon	White wine vinegar
1 cup water	Ricotta salata
¼ cup sugar	Olive oil
½ bunch purple asparagus	Black pepper
Flaky salt	

Slice large pieces of lemon peel, then boil them in the water and sugar for about 30 minutes. Let the peel cool in the syrup.

Trim the bottoms of the asparagus so no woody parts remain. Using a good vegetable peeler, strip the stalks, one long thin slice at a time. When you get to the tips, let them fall without attempting to peel them. Take the tips in your hands, then slice them down the middle. Maybe even quarter them if they are large.

Toss the asparagus strips and tips with fresh lemon juice and add a generous pinch of flaky salt. Dribble in some white wine vinegar. Toss again, then let sit for about 20 minutes.

In the meantime, grate the ricotta salata coarsely. Take out three wide strips of lemon peel from the syrup. Cut the lemon peel into long strips, then tinier pieces from there.

Set the asparagus over a fine-mesh sieve and push to release the extra liquid, or pick it all up and roll it in a paper towel. Taste; it should already be tender enough. If not enough lemon flavor remains, add more lemon juice.

Dress with the smallest amount of grassy olive oil and another pinch of flaky sea salt. Scatter with the ricotta salata and candied lemon peel, toss gently, season with loads of black pepper, then serve.

celery and walnut, with camembert + poppy seed crackers

I made this salad for the first time on a farm in down-east Maine, when Asher and Marit had arranged for me to cook a Secret Restaurant for their community out there. Tide Mill, the seventh-generation farm, had recently started a creamery. The creamery was producing ricotta, fromage blanc, and farmstead cream cheese. The cheesemaker, Rachel, was already starting to experiment with some blooming rind cheeses. Her first was a camembert, which she made four small wheels of, especially for this dinner. Presented with the challenge of making a dish celebrating this very special, smallest batch of cheese, I knew I wanted to serve it straight-up, with accompaniments. Celery is always wonderful with camembert, and they had all this tender young celery on the farm. Walnuts go beautifully with celery, so this simple salad came together. Then, a thick cracker laden with seeds, with a deep savor to it—something our grandmothers might have made.

Camembert

Vernal stalks of young celery

Walnut oil

Lemon juice

Salt

Black pepper

½ bunch (or hearty gathering) flat-leaf parsley

Walnuts

Poppy Seed Crackers (recipe follows)

Make sure to leave your camembert out of the fridge in order to bring it to room temperature.

Blanch the celery stalks whole in unsalted water for about 1 minute, to just barely tenderize them. Remove to an ice bath. When the celery is completely cool, remove each stalk and slice into thin, attractive strips. Pile these in a good salad bowl, then dress with walnut oil, lemon juice, salt, and pepper.

Wash and pull the tender stems off the tops of the parsley, about three-quarters of the way up, then mix in with the dressed celery.

(Continued)

Roast the walnuts at 375 degrees F for about 10 minutes, or until just starting to color a little. Once they cool, crush them with your fingers into the bowl with the celery.

Serve with a triangular wedge of camembert and the crackers.

POPPY SEED CRACKERS

---

1 cup (125 grams) all-purpose flour

½ cup (78 grams) whole wheat flour

¼ cup (28 grams) wheat germ

½ teaspoon (3 grams) fine salt

½ stick (58 grams) unsalted butter, cold and cut into about 30 small chunks

¼ cup (30 grams) poppy seeds

½ cup water

Milk

Flaky sea salt

Sift the flours, wheat germ, and fine salt together. Add the butter and, using your fingers, rub it into the flour mixture until it is in tiny bits and dispersed throughout.

Stir in the poppy seeds. Add the water and mix to make a stiff dough. Place on a lightly floured surface and roll out to about 8 by 10 inches. Cut into 20 squares. Place the dough squares on an ungreased baking sheet lined with parchment or foil. Brush sparingly with milk and sprinkle with sea salt. Bake at 300 degrees F for 30 minutes or until crisp but still pale. Transfer to a wire rack to cool and store in an airtight container for 2 to 3 weeks.

SNAPSHOTS OF EATING AND COOKING

My grandfather, a lifelong farmer and gardener, is eating tomatoes and fresh corn. The food dribbles around his chin, he smiles with glee and wipes his face with a napkin. The orange September sunlight streams through tall trees onto the back deck.

pickled cherries + pickled cherry tabbouleh

Tabbouleh was an oddly common dish on our table when I was growing up—for an Oregon-via-Midwest family, that is. My parents both just really like it, I guess. This version came to me after my first big batch of Pickled Cherries (page 71).

Sherried onions:	Parsley
Red onions	Mint
Sherry	Sage
Vinegar	2 lemons
	Pickled Cherries (recipe follows)
3 cups bulgur wheat	¾ cup olive oil
Almonds	Flaky salt
2 cucumbers	Black pepper

To make the sherried onions, slice an onion or two finely, place in a bowl, and cover with sherry and a few splashes of vinegar. Leave it to mellow for about 1 hour. Drain the onions before using, reserving the liquid for future salad dressings.

Soak the bulgur wheat in hot water for 10 to 15 minutes, or until it has bulked up, then fluff it with a fork.

(Continued)

While soaking the bulgur, toast and chop the almonds. Slice the cucumbers into long, thin slices with a vegetable peeler. De-stem and chop all the herbs. Roughly chop the sherried onions.

Zest and juice the lemons. Toss the bulgur with the pickled cherries, cucumbers, herbs, almonds, and sherried onions. Add the lemon juice, zest, and olive oil. Add flaky salt and black pepper to taste.

PICKLED CHERRIES

1 pound fresh cherries

¾ cup water

¾ cup distilled white vinegar

2 tablespoons white wine vinegar

1 tablespoon red wine vinegar

½ cup sugar

Dash of fine salt

1 heaping teaspoon whole black peppercorns

1 heaping teaspoon whole cardamom pods

1 heaping teaspoon juniper berries

1 heaping teaspoon coriander seeds

1 heaping teaspoon red pepper flakes

3 sprigs winter or summer savory, or 1 sprig rosemary

Stem and pit the cherries, reserving a few stones.

Put the water, vinegars, sugar, and salt in a tallish saucepan. Bring to a boil. Stir to dissolve the sugar and salt. Add the peppercorns, cardamom, juniper berries, coriander seeds, and red pepper flakes. Turn the heat gradually down to around medium and simmer for about 5 minutes.

Using a mesh strainer, strain the liquid into a bowl and then return to the clean pot over medium heat. Reserve the strained spices. Add the cherries and savory sprigs to the pot. Stir to coat the cherries with the liquid, cover, and increase the heat. When things are near a boil again, reduce to low and cook for a few minutes, or until the cherries have gone tender.

Put the reserved spices in the bottom of a clean quart mason jar. Turn off the heat, spoon the cherries into the jar, then cover with all the pickling liquid. Put a lid on the jar, put the jar in the fridge, wait a day or more, and enjoy. The cherries should keep for 1 month.

POTATO SALADS

parsley, anchovy, and olive oil mayonnaise potato salad

Sofie slipped a beautiful letterpress postcard with an olive oil mayonnaise recipe into a book she gave me shortly after we first met. It has lived on my fridge ever since, and frequently inspires dishes like this potato salad. It might have been brought on a picnic in France in the early 1900s, or Elizabeth David might have written about it, or maybe it is just the one I most often want to eat.

4 German butterball, Yukon Gold, or any new potatoes	½ batch Olive Oil Mayonnaise (recipe follows)
1 bunch curly parsley	Black pepper
4 anchovy fillets	Flaky salt

Halve the potatoes and boil in salted water until knife-tender. Remove to a medium bowl. Let cool before slicing them further into eighths.

Pull the parsley leaves from their stems and place in a small bowl. Remove half of them, chop finely and return, mixing the chopped parsley with the whole leaves.

Soak the anchovies if using salt-packed (though boquérones would be nice here). Debone them and cut into strips, then into pieces.

Toss the potatoes with the anchovy pieces to evenly distribute. The anchovy pieces should kind of stick to the potatoes. Distribute the mayonnaise, tossing gently. Dump in all the parsley and a crack of black pepper, then mix it all together. Top each serving with a generous dash of flaky salt.

OLIVE OIL MAYONNAISE

1 egg yolk, at room temperature

1 tablespoon tarragon white wine vinegar

1 teaspoon Dijon mustard

Pinch of salt

1 cup warm olive oil

Mix the egg yolk, vinegar, mustard, and salt together and add, drop by drop, the olive oil. Whisk steadily to emulsify. The mayonnaise should be enjoyed that day—have it at two meals! But it can be stored in a lidded jar in the refrigerator for 1 to 2 days.

french herb potato salad

For most people, potato salad is neither dull nor exciting, but I've always loved it and early on in my cooking life I strived to make it better and better. It's all in the timing of your preparation and your desire to make something that exceeds expectations. I once won a potato salad contest with this simple version. Variations on this formula are simple: use whatever herb combinations you fancy, switch between kinds of mayonnaise, or even try making it with sour cream instead.

---

6 to 8 Yukon Gold potatoes

All the herbs you can get your hands on

¼ to ½ cup olive oil

⅓ to ½ cup mayonnaise

Lemon juice

1 teaspoon white wine vinegar

Dijon mustard (optional)

Black pepper

Flaky salt

Bring generously salted water to a boil. Drop in the potatoes whole.

Put loads of de-stemmed herbs into a food processor (or Vitamix, if you are fancy and have one). Be sure to set aside some parsley and chervil. Glug in some olive oil (the amount will vary depending on how big of a potato salad you are making). Blitz, scrape down the sides, drop in a touch of water, blitz again.

Put mayonnaise (again, add amount based on the size of salad and your taste) in a bowl. Scrape the herby oil into the mayonnaise. Whisk to incorporate. Squeeze or drizzle in lemon juice. Add white wine vinegar. If more zing is needed, add Dijon mustard to taste.

When the potatoes are tender (poke with a fork to see), remove them from the water and let cool a bit. Mash partially with a potato masher. It is very important to add the herby mayonnaise at this point, while the potatoes are cooling off but still quite warm.

Let this sit for several minutes. Roughly chop the reserved parsley and chervil. Toss in the chopped herbs, season with loads of black pepper and flaky salt, then let cool further and enjoy at room temperature.

strawberry and sorrel potato salad

Lucas taught me about strawberry and sorrel. We were at our friend's farm in May. Lucas picked a few strawberries and some sorrel leaves. He invited us to eat them in one bite, insisting on how well it worked—"Like strawberry and rhubarb, but without the cooking." Some time later we made a really avant-garde tart for a Secret Restaurant dinner, using a dry-baked pie shell, lots of macerated strawberries, and ribbons of raw sorrel. Every time I eat the combination now, I remember the late afternoon May breeze as a group of us stood in the field, quietly enjoying the sweet and sour flavor party in our mouths.

Strawberries, at perfect ripeness	Sorrel, stems removed
Lemon juice	Oil
New potatoes (Red Gold or some variety with noteworthily gorgeous skin)	Labneh, Greek yogurt, crème fraiche, or fromage blanc
Salt	Black pepper
Mayonnaise (page 73 or highest quality store-bought)	Flaky salt

---

Delicately remove the green tops from the strawberries and slice thinly, discarding any over- or under-ripe parts you come across. Add a little lemon juice, cover, and leave to hang out for about 30 minutes.

Cook the potatoes whole in boiling salted water until tender to the prick of a fork. The new potatoes will cook quicker than those for the other potato salads in this book.

Drain the potatoes and let cool for 10 to 15 minutes. When they are cool enough to handle, chop into bite-size pieces, then toss with a couple spoonfuls of mayonnaise. This is an essential part of good potato salad. It's like adding the butter to mashed potatoes at just the right time!

Leave to cool the rest of the way, then salt to taste before moving forward.

Wash and dry the sorrel leaves, then stack and roll up in each other and slice into attractive ribbons. In a separate mixing bowl, dress them with the smallest amount of oil (any neutral oil is fine, walnut is lovely) and salt. Leave for about 10 minutes.

When ready to serve, move some potatoes to a new bowl, covering the bottom, making a first layer. Carefully add the strawberry slices to this layer of potatoes, scatter with sorrel leaves, toss with your salad-serving tools of choice, and repeat with the rest of the potatoes and sorrel leaves. Carefully dot large spoonfuls of labneh all over the top of the bowl before serving. Let each person aim for a serving with a big dollop of labneh, rather than letting it get pink in the bowl. This one is all about the delicacy of the flavors, and how it is eaten.

At the table, I suggest that each person adds a crack of black pepper and sprinkle of flaky salt.

italian deli, or "muffaletta," potato salad

My roommate Marta, who was often a guest for dinner as we shot this book, spent a long time staring into the distance while eating this potato salad. I wondered what she was thinking. "Muffaletta!" she exclaimed suddenly.

"What?" I asked.

"Muffaletta! Those Italian deli sandwiches. I was trying to remember what they were called. That's what this potato salad tastes like. In a good way!"

Purple potatoes	Castelvetrano olives (the unpitted kind always taste better and are worth the extra work)
Garlic	
Mildly spicy pickled peppers (Mama Lil's are perfect, other Italian-style peppers in oil are probably going to be good enough)	Arugula
	Fresh oregano or basil
Greek-style pepperoncini peppers	Olive oil
	Lemon juice
	Salt

Cook the potatoes whole in boiling salted water for 10 to 15 minutes. There will be a moment where the skin sort of cracks, but they will still hold together when a fork is inserted.

Drain the potatoes and let them cool for about 15 minutes. During this time, chop your garlic and peppers. Put the chopped garlic in a small bowl. Pour some of the pepperoncini pickling liquid over the garlic and leave for a few minutes to mellow it. Chop the olives but leave some in larger pieces (or whole if they are already pitted).

Stuff a food processor with the arugula and oregano, then pulse it several times. Chopping the herbs on a cutting board would be just fine too.

When the potatoes are cool enough to handle but still quite warm, cut them into bite-size pieces. Put the chopped potatoes in a mixing bowl, drizzle with lots of olive oil and toss. Add lemon juice and salt. Leave to cool the rest of the way, then combine with the olives, pickled peppers, pepperoncini peppers, and chopped herbs. Toss with more olive oil and lemon juice to taste. This salad is best served at room temperature, with grilled meat or vegetables, or perhaps picnic sandwiches.

SANDWICHES

pecorino fresco, pear, and frisée on kamut

This is a refined grilled cheese sandwich with a sweet and bitter edge.

Kamut or other ancient grain bread

Pecorino fresco or other semi-soft Italian or Spanish cheese

Butter

Pear (red D'anjou, if available)

Frisée

Black pepper

Slice the bread into medium-thick slices. Slice the cheese. Butter one side of the bread, set your favorite skillet over medium-low heat, and place the buttered side down in the pan. Top with half of the cheese.

After a few minutes, turn the heat down to low. When the bottom side is crisping slightly, lift with a flat spatula and set aside. Repeat the same process with the other side of the bread, flipping the reserved piece back onto it once the new one is settled in the pan.

Cook patiently! During this time, thinly slice the pear and wash and dry some leaves of frisée.

Continue to cook on low until the bread is golden brown and the cheese is oozing. When the sandwich is done, remove from the heat to a serving plate. Open the sandwich carefully with your hands. Stuff it with the pear (cracking on some black pepper is a nice touch) and frisée. Gently put it back together and eat, enjoying all the contrasts.

SNAPSHOTS OF EATING AND COOKING

A new Italian restaurant opens inside a house. We go during its first week. With a piece of the salt-less house-made Tuscan bread, I soak up green olive oil and black vinegar in a dish, eat, and am left speechless.

mushroom toastie

This is my interpretation of the Dutch grilled cheese sandwich. Serve it with a salad of bitter greens, lightly dressed with minced shallots, wine vinegar, and olive oil. Or with heavily herbed tomato soup, or one of lentils enlivened with toasted spices.

Good mustard

Good bread

Good butter

Good mushrooms

Good cheese

Spread good mustard on good bread. On the other side, spread the butter thinly. Work on a surface where it's okay to lay the butter side down for a while, like a wooden cutting board.

Flip on the broiler and place a cookie sheet in there to get hot.

Brush and trim the mushrooms. Keep them whole, and cook them in butter in a cast-iron pan. Press down to release their moisture. Flip them carefully. Don't crowd. Let the exteriors crisp a little.

Thickly grate some aged white cheddar, Gouda, Taleggio, or whatever delicious melting cheese you fancy. Sprinkle a layer on the mustard side of the bread. Pile the mushrooms over this layer, then top with another layer of cheese.

Pull out the hot baking sheet, using oven mitts, and set it down on the stove-top. Move the composed toasties from the work surface to the baking sheet. The butter should sizzle a little upon impact. Return the sheet to the oven and broil until the cheese bubbles, the bottom of the toastie is golden, and the whole thing is piping hot. Eat opened faced or press the two toasts together. Consider adding more mustard.

celery / tuna salad on walnut bread

I am one of those people who loves tuna sandwiches. Understandably, not everyone does—there are a lot of bad tuna sandwiches out there! Even if tuna salad has never been your thing, I encourage you to give this one a try. Kate prattled on about it for weeks after this shoot.

Durkee's Famous Sauce is the important "secret" ingredient here. It has the magical quality of tasting like deviled egg filling—it's mustardy, but richer, and has a flavor that is solid and substantial, yet less cloying than mayonnaise. The hint of vinegar is even a bit like white wine. It's an old-school sauce my mother introduced me to, and after my first taste I couldn't get enough. I had to search all around Portland to find it. Search your city—it is worth it.

Sweet onion	1 to 3 teaspoons Durkee's Famous Sauce
Celery (homegrown or from the farmers' market is best because then you get much fresher leaves)	Mayonnaise
	Dijon mustard
	Salt
Canned tuna in water (the wild-caught Oregon stuff if you can afford it)	Black pepper
	Walnut bread (your local best)

Slice the onion, then dice it somewhat aggressively. Wash, trim, and chop the celery in the same spot you chopped the onion so it soaks up some onion juices. Reserve any celery leaves.

Transfer the onion and celery to a mixing bowl, add in the tuna and its water (especially if you're using the good tuna), breaking up the chunks to your preference. The key ratio here is one to one, celery to tuna. It's important for texture and flavor.

Start with adding 1 teaspoon of Durkee's Famous Sauce, then adjust to your taste. I think I like it closer to 1 tablespoon. Add a little mayonnaise to offset the sharpness of the Durkee's, mix in with a fork, then adjust to taste with more Durkee's or Dijon mustard. Then season with salt and pepper. Throw in some torn celery leaves if you have them.

Toast the slices of walnut bread lightly, just enough to firm them up a bit, then let them cool. Pile the filling on generously and eat with salt and vinegar potato chips.

balik ekmek + ayran

In Istanbul, these sandwiches are served on boats bobbing on the Bosphorus, from little carts near the ferry, and from side windows of fish markets.

Before I went to Turkey, I didn't know much about it, and these fish sandwiches were actually the top thing that stuck in my mind from perusing travel guides. (Don't worry, I did have a life-changing visit to the Hagia Sofia, between sandwiches.)

Mackerel is the recommended fish, if you can get it in your area. In the Northwest it's actually not very common. It is around in the early summer though. It's cheap and so, so good. Trout and rockfish are also good options.

A whole fish will make a couple sandwiches, or plan on one fillet per sandwich. The idea is that you have plenty of fish. The name of the sandwich, balik ekmek, translates to "fish bread." That said, if you are serving this with many other courses or sides, you can split the sandwiches and serve each person a half.

Mackerel, trout, or other white fish

Flaky salt

Lemon, juice and zest

Poblano or other peppers, or some other favorite flavorful vegetable for grilling

Olive oil

Black pepper

Garlic

Farmstead cream cheese, fromage blanc, or any other favorite spreadable, mild-yet-tangy cheese

Wide demi-baguette or any favorite sandwich roll

Bottled lemon juice (optional)

Strong peppery greens (green radicchio, arugula, mustard greens, escarole)

Ayran (recipe follows)

If using a whole fish, clean and gut it. (This can be gruesome if you aren't used to doing it or don't have the proper tools, but is totally worth getting used to and getting the proper tools. I have one fish knife bought at a Vietnamese grocery five years ago, used only for cutting fish. So most of the time it's wrapped in a cloth and kept tucked away.) Cut from the bottom seam of the fish (you'll see it) up to the head. Take a pair of scissors and make cuts away from the center on either side of the head, like a Y shape. Use a knife to cut off the head. Repeat the process in the other direction, removing the tail. Being careful not to smash the flesh, scrape the guts out onto an easy-to-sanitize surface (like

(Continued)

the sink basin). Cut the fish the rest of the way open, until you have two long fillets. Wash under gently running cold water. If large bone pieces seem easily removable, cut them off. Mackerel debones easier when cooked, so if you are using that, wait to pull out the main skeleton.

Sprinkle the fillets with flaky salt and lemon juice on both sides, and cover with foil.

Toss the peppers with olive oil, salt, and black pepper. Peel the garlic, then slice thinly to about $\frac{1}{6}$ inch. Lay the slices on a cutting board, and brush both sides with oil. To prepare the spread, mix the lemon zest with the cheese. Wash the salad leaves and set them aside.

Cook everything on the same surface, ideally a long-ridged cast-iron grill pan set over two burners. A large cast-iron pan works great too. Or an outdoor grill!

Heat the grilling surface on high. If it isn't oily, brush with oil. Drop the peppers on. Turn on your kitchen fan. Let them puff up and char on one side. Turn the heat down to medium. Using tongs, carefully turn the peppers over to char the other side.

Take them off the heat and put them in a covered dish. Lower the heat to medium low and add the garlic slices. Cook each side for about one and a half minutes, being careful to not let them burn. The flesh will go from opaque to vaguely translucent. Remove and put them in the covered dish with the peppers.

If the grill pan is oily enough, don't bother adding oil, but if it seems to be drying out, brush the skin side of the fish with oil.

Lay the fish fillets carefully, skin side down, on the pan. As they spit and crackle a little, slide a spatula under and move them around a bit to ensure that they don't stick. Most of the cooking is done on the skin side. You'll notice it start to crisp up. After about 2 or 3 minutes, the fillets are probably ready to flip.

Flip the fillets, and cook for about 45 seconds. Flip over again to the skin side to finish cooking. After a minute or two back on the skin side, they should be just done and meltingly tender. Flake off a piece of flesh to test for doneness. Remove the bones, either during the last minute on the grill or once taken off the heat. The guys in Turkey have an incredible way of pulling the bones out at this stage using nothing but tongs and a flick of the wrist. Sometimes I can do it, with tongs and a fork, but other times I wait until the fish is off the grill.

Pull gently, from the thick center of the spine, and the bones should come out easily. Work gently with a fork or your hands if you need to.

Move the fillets to a lidded baking pan to keep them warm. Slice your demi-baguette in half and place on the grill, cut-side down. Turn the heat up. Press down on them after a minute or so to encourage the toasting.

When the bread is just a bit grilled and warmed through, turn off the heat and quickly assemble the sandwich. Spread the cheese on the bottom half of the bread. Place the fish on top. Squeeze a lemon or drizzle bottled lemon juice (it tastes different, with the presence of lemon oil, and is what they use in Turkey) generously over the fish. Douse it even. Throw some more flaky salt on if you like. Lay the pieces of grilled garlic and peppers on top of the fish. Put the greens on last. Close and devour while still hot, sipping cold ayran between bites.

(Continued)

AYRAN

One part high-quality plain active live-culture yogurt

One part water

¼ to 1 teaspoon fine sea salt

Put the yogurt into a glass measuring cup—you want one with a milliliter reading on it. Once measured, move the yogurt to a pitcher or tall bowl. Measure out an equal amount of water and pour it in with the yogurt. Add salt to taste: start with ¼ teaspoon no matter how much yogurt you are using and adjust from there. Better safe than too salty. As a guide, think of the saltiness of the drink like seasoning the dish. You want it to help bring out the flavor of whatever food you're eating while drinking it, not detract from it.

Using an immersion blender, blend until smooth. You can also do all this business in some kind of smoothie contraption or with a handheld beater. Be careful if using a food processor, as it could easily end up too messy. Taste and adjust salt as desired.

This can be served with fresh mint or other herbs, smacked with the back of a knife to release their oils and stuffed into the glass. I prefer it pretty straight up. It's designed to be a filling, nourishing palate cleanser. I like to make a batch of this and store it in a fancy beverage container like a Weck juice jar or a pop-top glass bottle.

roasted tomato, anchovy, and feta pocket sandwich

It was my first and only time in Paris; I had been walking for hours, so far disappointed by the food. A door opened on a random side street, someone spilled out and walked away. I caught a glimpse of the inside and saw Henry Miller's 1930s Paris in one glance and was sucked in. I smelled the wood fire and saw a chalkboard menu of five euro sandwiches. Soon I was handed half of a rustic loaf stuffed with roasted tomatoes, anchovies, and sheep's milk feta, then stuck in the oven until slightly charred and bubbling hot. I went back out into the streets and ate the hot, beautiful sandwich. Then, of course, it rained.

Canned tomatoes, drained	Anchovy fillets
Olive oil	French sheep's milk feta
Black pepper	A good sandwich roll

Toss the tomatoes with olive oil and black pepper. Roast the tomatoes in at 500 degree F for 15 to 20 minutes, or until they get sticky and caramelized. Wash and debone the anchovies (or take them out of the oily jar) and crumble the feta.

Stuff the rolls with the roasted tomatoes, anchovies, and cheese, then them pop back in the blazing hot oven until the edges have crisped.

DINNERS

sushi bowl (for the cold months)

This recipe was conceived during a stretch of cooking Japanese-inspired dishes on cold January nights, "cleansing" after the holidays. Though it is filling and rich-tasting, the clean, bright flavors feel healthful and restorative.

Tofu (extra-firm if available)

1 cup sushi rice

2 cups water

High-heat frying oil

Ginger, a piece the size of your thumb

1 slim Japanese eggplant per person, or 1 large globe eggplant

Oyster sauce

Ponzu

Mirin (high quality if you can find it; this is an ingredient where I notice a difference.)

Umeboshi plum vinegar

1 sheet nori of per person

At least 1 maitake mushroom per person

Tamari

Pickled ginger

Bonito flakes (optional)

Cut the tofu into long slices ¾ inch thick. Cut these slices into bite-size triangles (roughly 4 per person). Place on a lined baking sheet and stick in the freezer. After 15 minutes, check them, turning the pieces over to freeze on all sides.

Wash the rice thoroughly under cold water. Make five or six passes, until the water runs clear. Drain, combine with the water in a rice cooker, and proceed with other aspects of the meal.

Get a deep saucepan with a tight-fitting lid and fill it with approximately 1 inch of oil and heat the oil over high heat. Meanwhile, peel and chop the ginger. With a straining tool, lower the ginger into the hot oil and hold it there for about 30 seconds. It will take some of the bite out of the ginger and infuse the oil. Remove and set aside as a garnish for the sushi bowl or save for another use.

When the oil is super hot but not smoking and the tofu is frozen, get the tofu out. Take the lid in one hand and, using tongs, pick up a tofu piece with the other hand. Drop the tofu into the hot oil and immediately slam the lid down over the pot. It will be very loud as the water erupts in the oil, but delectable pockets are forming inside the tofu as the frozen water explodes. The outsides go appetizingly chewy, the insides are soft and textured more like chicken than usual.

When the popping simmers down, repeat the process with the rest of the tofu pieces. After a minute or two, when the pan is starting to get full, the first piece will definitely be done on one side. Find it and flip it with the tongs. Turn the heat down momentarily if you need to, then crank it up again once all the pieces have been flipped. Watch carefully—you don't want them to get overly brown.

Remove the tofu pieces to a paper towel to drain. Try to keep them warm, in a lidded dish or perhaps a toaster oven on low. Chop the eggplants into bite-size pieces.

If the oil has any tofu pieces that have broken off and burned, clear it out with your strainer. Then add the eggplant, cut side down, to the hot oil. More eggplant can go in the oil at once. When the cut sides start to turn golden, about 2 to 3 minutes, flip the pieces with the tongs. You want them to get appetizingly brown. Pull them out when it feels right and they have clearly "given." Drain, then toss with oyster sauce and ponzu. Keep hot, in a lidded dish or perhaps a toaster oven on low. They aren't done yet.

Around this time the rice should be done. Attend it to it, taking the lid off, adding a glug of mirin, stirring with the paddle, then drizzling in 1 tablespoon of umeboshi plum vinegar. Tear up the nori.

Heat a dry cast-iron pan over medium-high heat, add the fried and dressed eggplant and gently finish by reheating and crisping it a little.

Meanwhile, set the maitakes in a roasting tin. Drizzle with oyster sauce, tamari, plum vinegar, and mirin. Roll the mushrooms around in the sauces that they didn't absorb. Put the tin under the broiler. Take it out after about 3 minutes and press down on the mushrooms with a spatula to let out some of the moisture. Roll them around in the sauces again. Return to the broiler. Keep a close eye. They will need a minute or two more to start browning and crisping around the edges. Remove when the mushrooms are tender but the coral-like edges are like the crisped outer skin of a pork chop.

(*Continued*)

Divide the rice into bowls and toss with torn pieces of nori and pieces of pickled ginger. Stick the tofu in among the rice. Add the eggplant and the maitakes when they are smoking hot and ready to eat. Drizzle with more of the seasoning sauces to taste. I like the stark contrast of the separate flavors, but you can also tear up and toss the tofu with the eggplant and maitakes to coat everything in the sauces before adding to the bowls. Throw on some bonito flakes if you're into the wavy thing.

sushi bowl (for the warmer months)

Summers in Oregon are very dry and—contrary to popular belief—long and hot. I often find myself wanting to eat nothing but experimental sushi bowls for days and days.

1 cup sushi rice

2 cups water

Mirin

Rice and/or umeboshi plum vinegar

1 large or 2 medium cucumbers

Salt

Ponzu

1 large fresh sardine or other favorite fresh, smoked, or tinned fish (optional)

Oil

1 knob of ginger

A handful of pea shoots and purslane (or whatever seasonal greens, herbs, or veggies you like) per person

Lemon or bottled lemon juice

1 large avocado

Fish sauce

Tamari

Sweet soy sauce

Pickled ginger

1 sheet of nori per person

Gomashio or other sesame/seaweed rice topping

Wash the rice six times (yes, six times) under cold water, or until the water runs clear. Drain, combine with the water in a rice cooker and proceed with other aspects of the meal. Consider making more rice than you need for this recipe. Having cold sticky rice around for a day or two is great.

(Continued)

Once the rice is done, spread it in a wide dish to let the steam out, drizzling some mirin and rice vinegar over it and stirring as you go. Pop it into the freezer for 5 minutes. When you take it out and toss again, the rice should be perfectly cool.

Chop the cucumber into cubes and dress with a little salt, mirin, and ponzu. Set aside.

This recipe was originally a way to use up some fresh sardines that had been cooked the day before. (Sushi bowls are always a great way to use up extra fish. You'll be dressing it, and you want it cold anyway.) If you're starting from scratch, heat a grill pan on high. If you bought cleaned fish, just split them down the center to make two halves. If you are starting with a truly whole fish, gut and bone the sardine (instructions for this are in Balik Ekmek + Ayran on page 88). Rub both sides of the sardine with oil and sprinkle salt on the skin side. Grill skin side down until the fish starts to puff up. When this happens, the fish is about three-quarters of the way done. Agitate with a spatula, then flip. Only grill the second side for about 45 seconds. Flip back onto the skin side to crisp a moment longer. From this state, flake pieces of the finished fish into a bowl, deboning as you go.

Peel and chop the fresh ginger. Use a small frying pan to cook it for about 30 seconds in a flavor-neutral oil. Toss the gingery oil and ginger with the cooled rice.

Snip the pea shoots and purslane with scissors into the rice. Squeeze half a lemon over it or add a glug or two of bottled lemon juice.

Add the dressed cucumber and toss. Add the flaked fish and toss. Slice the avocado, add it, and toss. Dress the whole bowl with ponzu, fish sauce, tamari, sweet soy sauce, and mirin to your liking. Add pieces of pickled ginger.

Tear or crumble in the nori, and toss once more. Sprinkle with the gomashio.

SNAPSHOTS OF EATING AND COOKING

On a farm in New Hampshire, my friends and I have the dream of a '60s/'70s-style farm and artists' community. It is three in the afternoon. I stop building the deck, drop the hammer, wash my head with cold water under the outdoor shower, then walk through the garden picking. I head down to the open makeshift kitchen, garage door flung open to let in the breeze. Alone with the buzzing of insects and the clank of hammers in the distance, I quietly cook dinner for everyone, so happy to be living the slow life.

udon, tofu, glazed carrots, chrysanthemum

Sometimes the best dinner is a giant bowl of sticky, heavily seasoned noodles and vegetables. Edible chrysanthemum is very easy to grow, so for a while I've had it in my garden. Look out for it at farmers' market stalls or Asian grocery stores. You can also easily substitute pretty much any cooking green—perhaps mustards or bok choy would be the most appropriate.

4 to 6 carrots, depending on size	Sugar
1 (10-ounce) roll dry udon noodles	Mirin
½ block firm tofu	Ponzu
Canola oil	Tamari
Ground ginger	Generous handfuls of edible chrysanthe-
Fish sauce	mum leaves and tender stalks or other greens of your choice

Boil water for the carrots and the noodles. Use a wide, deep-rimmed pan (rather than a soup pot) if you have one. Before cooking the noodles, wash and trim the carrots. Cut them down the center and divide into two pieces each. Drop them in the boiling water for just 1 minute. Remove to a separate bowl and immediately wash twice in cold water to stop them from cooking further.

Now cook the noodles for 10 minutes while working on other aspects of the dish. When they are ready, pause to tip them into a colander and set aside.

Slice the tofu into large ½-inch-thick squares. Take each of those squares and cut them diagonally down the center to make triangles. If you have time to let them drain on towels, great, but if not it's okay. Plunge ahead (wearing an apron, maybe, to protect against possible splattering).

Heat your best thin-bottomed nonstick frying pan and add a layer of canola oil. When the oil shimmers, slide the tofu triangles in, using a thin spatula and a fork to guide them gently. Let them sizzle actively for about 1 minute, then agitate each one slightly to make sure they aren't sticking. Cook, patiently, for 3 to 5 minutes. Watch the edges start to brown and crisp, check the bottoms with the spatula, then flip them over. Cook the other side for about 2 minutes, until browned but slightly less so than the first side. Remove from the pan, onto a baking dish, and immediately sprinkle both sides with ground ginger, smoothing to coat with the back of a spoon. Dribble over some fish sauce on both sides. This is the best quick tofu, and works with many other dishes!

Tip most of the excess oil from the pan into a wok, wide-rimmed frying pan, or even a shallow soup pot. Return the frying pan to the stove. Roll the carrots in the remaining oil still hanging out there. Toss the tiniest amount of sugar in with them too. Lay the carrots, cut side down, in the pan and turn the heat back to medium. Cook patiently until the cut edges begin to caramelize, then swiftly remove the carrots to the baking dish with the tofu.

Heat the wok (or other pan) with its little pool of oil in the bottom, and add a generous splash of mirin. Have the chrysanthemum or other cooking greens handy. Add the drained noodles in stages so they don't stick too quickly, turning and scraping with a wooden spatula the whole time. After all the noodles are in the pan, add some splashes of ponzu and tamari. Drop in all the greens at once, tossing vigorously to steam and cook them. It will take only a little over 1 minute for the greens to brighten and tenderize. Drop in the tofu and carrots to reheat and distribute them. Arrange in a bowl with the tofu circling the noodles, carrots, and greens. Add more ponzu and tamari to taste.

all flower salad

If you have access to a large quantity of edible flowers (like, you grow them) then this is an excellent thing to serve next to heavier main courses. I like it tremendously with Japanese-ish food.

Delicate, spicy flowers with light dressing. The quantities here for the dressing are for each individual serving, so scale up as needed.

½ teaspoon oil

1 teaspoon mirin

¼ teaspoon rice vinegar

¼ teaspoon ponzu

A medium plate or salad bowl's worth of edible flowers per person

To make the dressing, stir the oil, mirin, rice vinegar, and ponzu vigorously.

Delicately pick and arrange the flowers on each plate. Washing would wilt them, so don't! Just drizzle half the dressing over them, toss as gently as you can, drizzle the rest, toss that, and enjoy its depth of flavor.

hearty dinner salad (spring version)

Inspired by some substantial salads from a favorite Portland Farmers Market food vendor, this dinner salad can be altered and adapted quite easily for any season. One could add beans, or make a tahini dressing rather than a yogurt dressing, or switch out vegetables for the best of whatever season you are in. Make sure to consider the textures!

1½ cups wheat berries

Vegetable stock

2 large handfuls of fresh shelling peas

Salt

4 or 5 small new potatoes

Grassy olive oil

4 or 5 small white spring turnips

1 large purple daikon or watermelon radish

Umeboshi plum or other good vinegar

4 or 5 stalks celery

½ bunch parsley

Green garlic, a few stems

2 bunches spinach

Dressing:

Good live culture yogurt

Garlic or onion powder, or fancy green garlic powder (there is a recipe in *Bar Tartine* by Nicolaus Bala and Cortney Burns)

White pepper

Lemon juice

Flaky salt

Soak the wheat berries overnight. Drain, and set them to cook in a tall saucepan or soup pot, with enough vegetable stock to cover the wheat berries by about 1 inch. Bring to a boil, stir, then reduce to a simmer and cover, cooking for 1½ to 2 hours. When the liquid is mostly, if not completely, absorbed and the wheat berries are puffed up, tasty, and tender from the stock, they are ready. Set aside to cool.

Shell all the peas into a separate bowl. Boil water rapidly, adding a dash of salt, then the peas. Set a timer for a minute and a half. Prepare a small ice bath in the bowl the peas just came out of. Pull out the peas with a slotted spoon or strainer, and add them to the ice bath. Add your new potatoes to the boiling salted water. Cook for 5 to 8 minutes, or until they give to the prodding of a fork. Drain and set aside, dressing lightly with salt and a little grassy olive oil.

Slice the turnips into ⅙-inch coins. Slice the radishes as thinly as possible. Lay out the radish and turnip slices on separate plates. Sprinkle with salt, leave for several minutes, then top with a healthy sprinkling of umeboshi plum vinegar. Leave to lightly pickle.

Wash and trim the celery, then cut it into pleasing, bite-size matchstick pieces. Drain the peas from the ice bath and toss them with the celery.

(Continued)

Wash and dry the parsley, then pull off the tops, including the tender upper stems (discard the lower stems or save them for stock). Chop roughly and add to the celery and peas. Thinly slice the green garlic, adding it to the bowl as well.

Wash the first bunch of spinach. Heat a large pan over high heat, then add the slightly wet spinach and actively turn over and over with tongs until it has cooked down and is bright green. Add a sprinkling of salt and turn over once again. Remove and repeat with the second bunch. When it has all cooked down and cooled, pick up the bundle of wet spinach with your hands and squeeze the excess moisture out into the sink.

Make the dressing in a separate small bowl or measuring cup, stirring the garlic powder and white pepper into the yogurt and getting the yogurt to a very smooth consistency. If it is too thick to pour, thin it with kefir, cream, milk, or water.

In a large bowl, combine the cooked wheat berries and spinach, turnips, radishes, celery, shelling peas, green garlic, and parsley leaves. Sprinkle lemon juice and flaky salt over it all, then toss. In the individual bowls, pool the dressing in the center of the salad, and serve.

clams, ramps, bread

Eat this dish fast. Pull clams out of their shells and press them into
the grilled side of the bread. Lay ramps over the clams. Then, making
room in the bowl, lower the untoasted side of the bread into the
clam jus and let it soak a little. Devour the whole thing in a few bites.
Repeat if this is your dinner on a rainy spring night, or serve this as a
starter course where everyone gets a little to really excite the appetite.

Clams (if you are on either coast, try to find local clams)	A medium oval loaf of bread
	Porcini or truffle salt or any extra-flavorful salt (optional)
White wine	
Butter	Ramps or bunching onions, or young cultivated leeks

Wash the clams to remove sandy bits, discarding any with broken shells. Place
them in a lidded saucepan with a splash of water and a heavy splash of white
wine. Heat over medium heat, partially covered. Check regularly after 2 or
3 minutes; cook for as long as 5 to 7. It shouldn't take longer than that for the
clams to open. If they don't, they should be discarded.

While the clams are cooking, melt a big pat of butter in a glass measuring cup.

When most of the clams have opened, turn off the heat and close the lid firmly.

Heat a cast-iron pan on high. Slice your bread into long pieces. Using a pastry
brush, brush one side with the melted butter. Set the slices butter side down
directly in the pan. Using another pan or some other weight, press the bread
into the pan to char it slightly.

While the bread toasts, act quickly and grab a good dish for the clams. Put the
clams and clam jus in the dish along with a spoonful of the melted butter.

Remove the bread from the pan and turn off the heat. If you have any mushroomy salt—porcini or truffle salt—this bread is a great place to sprinkle it.

Trim the very bottoms from the ramps. Using the pastry brush, dress them
lightly with the remaining melted butter. The bread pan should still be quite
hot. Drop the ramps in. Press down on the ends with a spatula to get them
to char a bit. When the leaves are just wilting and they seem cooked through
and on the threshold of burning, take them out of the pan and put them
straight into the serving dish with the clams. Tuck the pieces of grilled bread
in around the clams and ramps.

spring onion / turnip tart

I love cooking spring turnips gently in butter, and I love savory pie. I hope you do too, or that you make this dish and start to. Caña de oveja is a Spanish goat cheese with a soft, delectable rind. You could use any soft goat cheese successfully here.

½ cup (1 stick) butter, plus more for the turnips

1 cup sage leaves, plus more for garnish

1½ cups all-purpose flour

Good salt

5 to 6 tablespoons ice water4 or 5 spring (Hakurei) turnips

Spring onions (a bunch of small, a couple of medium, or one large—best yet, calçots, the Spanish bunching spring onions)

Oil

Caña de oveja or other favorite goat cheese

Labneh or cultured cream cheese, crème fraîche, or full-fat plain yogurt

Rosemary flowers (optional)

To make the tart crust, freeze the butter (or at least put it in the freezer for a while before starting). Chop the sage leaves.

In a food processor or large bowl, combine the flour, a pinch of good salt and the chopped sage leaves. Cut the chilled butter into small pieces, crumbling as you go and dropping them in with the flour. Blitz four or five times until the mixture is quite pebbly.

If using a food processor, transfer to a large bowl. Add the ice water, 1 table-spoon at a time, incorporating with a wooden spoon. When you can form the dough into a ball, do so, and refrigerate for 1 hour, or freeze until you're actually going to make the tarts. Take out the dough with plenty of time to defrost or adjust to room temperature. When it is ready, roll it out into a large sheet and cut out circles for your tarts, tracing around your pans or ramekins and adding an inch all around the sides to compensate for a bit of shrinking that will happen during baking. Shape the tarts and place them in the freezer until ready to fill and bake.

To prepare the turnips, bring a pan of water deep enough to submerge them to a boil. Trim the tops and stringy bits. Drop the turnips, whole, into the water. Let them bubble away for 8 to 15 minutes. When tender to the touch of a knife, remove them and drop into a bowl of cold water. After a minute or two, drain off this now warm water, refill with more cold water, and repeat until the turnips are at room temperature.

(Continued)

Slice them thinly into ¼-inch discs. Drop some butter into the same pan you just used, now drained of the water. The residual heat will do most of the work. Turn the heat to low and add the turnips. Cook for a minute or two, turn off the heat, cover, and let the turnips continue absorbing the butter. Leave the pan on the stove, as you'll be adding the onions in a few minutes.

To prepare the spring onions, slice into discs and then chop roughly. Don't be concerned about uniformity! Get a cast-iron grill pan or other favorite pan really hot. Drop in a small glug of oil. Working in batches, add the onions making sure to fill the pan but not to overcrowd it. Let them be for a minute or two, sprinkle with salt, then press down on them with a flat spatula. This will release a bunch of the moisture and help them to break down. The green bits will go bright, the bottoms will brown. Stir briefly, continue cooking a little bit longer, then tip them in with the turnips and cook another batch.

To assemble the tarts, crumble the goat cheese into a bowl (including its supple rind if you're using caña de oveja). Add the labneh and stir together vigorously. Add the cheese mixture to the onions and turnips, stirring gently (mostly so that you don't break the pieces of turnip). Scrape the mixture into your prepared crusts. Top each tart with a single sage leaf. It should crisp delightfully.

Bake at 425 degrees F for 25 to 35 minutes. The tarts are done when the edges are golden and the top is bubbling and crisping in places. Top with rosemary flowers if you have access to some.

Serve with a small salad of whatever flavorful green you fancy or have around.

dry eggplant parmesan

I love a well-prepared classic eggplant Parmesan, soaking in red sauce with bubbling cheese on top. I even love a mediocre one, kind of soggy and forgettable but warm and filling on a winter night. The really, really good preparations have a moment where you bite through the crisp breading into the creamy umami-blast interior, even through the sauce. I came up with this version when I had a craving for the classic but only had thin eggplants from my home garden to use and a precious last cup of all-garden tomato sauce. I imagined making the eggplant with perfect, Parmesan-y crust, then cutting a piece and sliding it through that tomato sauce. Far from the "eggplant whatever" dishes listed at the bottom of meat-centric menus, this is a dish you really can luxuriate over, knife-and-forking succulent mouthfuls with delicious sauces.

1 or 2 small to medium Japanese eggplants per person

Salt

Olive oil

Black pepper

Balsamic vinegar

Best possible bread crumbs (as in 3 days ago you had some awesome naturally leavened bread you didn't finish, then you blitzed the rest of it in the food processor for this recipe)

Lots of freshly grated Parmesan (go for affordable Wisconsin Parmesan here; I also really enjoy mixing finer Parmesan with Trader Giotto's cheap Parmesan)

Roughly 1 eggs per person to start, plus more if needed

All-purpose flour, for dredging

Fresh mozzarella or burrata

Creamy Pesto Sauce (page 117)

Candied Tomato Puttanesca (page 116)

Trim the tops of the eggplants and cut them lengthwise into halves. Score each half diagonally and deeply with a small, sharp knife. Sprinkle with salt and set in a colander in the sink to drain for 15 to 30 minutes. If you don't have time for this, it's okay, but it does help them absorb the olive oil in the right way.

Marinate the eggplant with plenty of olive oil, salt, pepper, and a dash or two of balsamic vinegar. Toss to coat and set aside. A long Pyrex casserole dish is the perfect vessel for this. Half an hour should be plenty of time. Make that salad! Or the pesto!

Heat a cast-iron pan (or two, if you are cooking for lots of people) over medium-high heat. Glug in some olive oil, then add the eggplant pieces, cut

(Continued)

sides down. After a minute or so, agitate to ensure that they don't stick, but don't flip them yet.

When the cut sides are turning golden, flip them over and cook on the skin sides. If the other sides are done enough, they should puff up here for a moment. Using a metal spatula, press the edges down to encourage this. They are growing tender on each side without getting mushy. The flesh should now start looking less opaque. Poke the pieces with gentle force—you'll see the last of the moisture escaping and bursting into little steam clouds next to the eggplants. This will steam the eggplants through to doneness. When they are just done, before they collapse further, remove them from the heat and return them to the dish where they marinated.

Arrange three flat dishes near the stove. Mix the bread crumbs with the Parmesan in one, beat the eggs in another, and spread the flour in the last. If the bread crumbs are from really good, naturally leavened sourdough bread, they will have so much flavor and don't need further seasoning. If they aren't, that's okay—but maybe add some herbs, garlic, or chili powder. Semolina flour is nice too and can be mixed however you like with the plain flour, if you want to sneak in some other flavor.

Clean the cast-iron pan from the stove and ready to go again, setting it over medium heat with a thin layer of oil.

Make the pieces of eggplant Parmesan one at a time. First, roll each eggplant piece in flour. The oil on it from previous cooking should make the flour coat it properly. Then dip it in the egg. Then roll, dip, or set in/sprinkle with the bread crumb and Parmesan mixture. Dip in the egg mixture again. Repeat with the bread crumb and Parmesan mixture. This thick layer is what you want, but make sure it's sticking reasonably well before you start throwing it in the pan. Do you need more egg mixture? Maybe. Fewer bread crumbs? Maybe. Get a sense of how it's going, then gently set the piece of eggplant in the pan, cut side down. Repeat with one or two pieces, then check the first piece (using a pair of tongs). When a nice crust is forming and you can easily lift it, turn it over and cook the other side in the same way. Remove to a paper or clean kitchen towel to drain as you go.

After a minute or two, the eggplant pieces will do all the draining they are going to do and you should then transfer them to baking sheets or dishes set in a 250-degree-F oven. Let them hang out in there for at least 15 minutes (30 minutes if you have the time). In the oven they will dry up on the outside and grow more tender on the inside.

A few minutes before serving, top the pieces in the oven with the mozzarella. Let it start to melt, then broil it for 1 final minute before serving. Try them with a side of spaghetti, Candied Tomato Puttanesca, and Creamy Pesto Sauce, or any other favorites of yours. Eat the pieces of exquisite eggplant like a steak, one forkful at a time, dipped in sauce.

candied tomato puttanesca

This emulates the same method as for the Candied Tomatoes on page 186. One time I was starting to make puttanesca on the stovetop, then realized all of a sudden that it would be interesting to put all the ingredients in a baking dish and prepare it that way, tucking fresh oregano in at the end for a strong, herbaceous lift. This is great with eggplant Parmesan, with any pastas (but it is particularly awesome with rigatoni or cheese ravioli), with polenta, with beans, or with a fun and indulgent appetizer, like homemade garlic knots or breadsticks! Those could easily be improvised from Pizza Dough, White and Wheat (page 132).

---

2 pints best cherry tomatoes

5 to 6 cloves garlic

1 or 2 anchovy fillets

Olive oil

Salt

4 to 5 caper berries (regular capers will do just fine)

Handful of fresh oregano leaves

Remove the stems from the cherry tomatoes and cut them in half. Put in a baking dish. Peel and thinly slice the garlic. Arrange it around the tomatoes.

If the anchovy is salt-packed, wash and debone it, then chop it. If oil-packed, just chop it. Tuck those pieces around the tomatoes as well. Drizzle with loads of olive oil and sprinkle with a little salt.

Bake at 400 degrees F for 30 minutes. Remove and stir. Lower the heat to 350 degrees F and bake for another 30 minutes. Remove and stir. Chop up the caper berries, add them, and return the dish to the oven. Lower the heat to 300 degrees F and bake for another 30 minutes. Remove and add the fresh oregano leaves to the sizzling, candied tomatoes.

creamy pesto sauce

Everyone should make pesto whenever they desire it and with whatever garlic, herbs, leaves, nuts, and cheese are available to them. This recipe is an example of how you can get a little experimental and still yield a sauce that works in any context. This one is great with the Dry Eggplant Parmesan (page 113), with pasta, on polenta, as a sandwich spread, and as a salad dressing.

A small handful raw almonds

3 to 6 cloves of garlic

Enough basil to fill your food processor's chamber

Olive oil or almond oil

Salt

Black pepper

Handful of Parmesan

3 or 4 spoonfuls full-fat European-style plain yogurt

½ teaspoon water

Blanch the almonds: pour boiling water over them in a bowl, let sit for 90 seconds, drain the water, then peel the skins under cold running water.

Peel the garlic. Put the garlic and almonds in the bottom of the food processor. Tear the basil off its stems and add it as well. Drizzle with olive oil (or almond oil, if you have it around), then blitz until a paste begins to form.

Scrape down the sides, add another generous glug of olive oil, generous pinches of salt and pepper, the Parmesan, yogurt, and water. Blitz again, leaving the food processor running long enough to get the almonds to an extremely smooth consistency within the sauce. You may want to add a little more yogurt or olive oil halfway through. Keep tasting and adjusting until the end result is creamy, tangy, zingy, and delicious.

hearty dinner salad (fall version)

I go into the kitchen at work during my ten-minute break and tear the leaves with my hands. I cut a piece of lemon and squeeze the juice over the kale with a little salt. I whip up whatever that day's version of tahini dressing will be (harissa? garlic? lemon? ponzu?), crudely chop vegetables, toss it all in a mixing bowl, and eat the salad with a hunk of bread on the side. This salad is what came from thinking about making that haphazard, delicious lunch into a complete, considered, and special seasonal dinner.

Slightly heaping ½ cup wild rice

Scant ½ cup long-grain brown rice

1¾ cups water

Butter

Olive oil

Flaky salt

4 or 5 small red potatoes

1 onion

½ bunch lacinato kale plus a few leaves of purple kale, if you have it around (any combination of kales works fine)

Lemon juice

1 extra beautiful carrot

Tarragon white wine vinegar

1 ripe persimmon

½ ripe pear

2 medium lobster mushrooms (if you can't find them, try other wild mushrooms, or torn roasted chicken or duck)

3 tablespoons tahini

Whatever herbs or seasonings sound good (for this salad, don't do garlic; it won't work with the persimmon)

For the crispy rice, first wash the rices 3 or 4 times under cold running water. Combine them with the water and 1 tablespoon butter or oil in a rice cooker, or cook on the stovetop according to your preferred method. When the rice is done, spread it out on a cold metal baking sheet. The addition of a splash of apple cider vinegar will help bring the rice together if it cooks dry. Place the baking sheet somewhere to cool, preferably outside of the warm kitchen.

When the rice has cooled, separate it into small clumps about the size of croutons. Squeeze the pieces together with your hands, if necessary, to keep their shape. Heat a cast-iron pan (or two) with a glug of olive oil over medium-high heat. Once hot, drop the clumps of rice in and leave them there to fry for a minute or two. The brown rice turning an appetizing golden brown is the perfect indicator that it's time to flip. The resulting pieces should be crispy all around but still tender on the inside. Crush a finger full of flaky salt over the finished pieces as you remove them from the pan. You can season them any way you like; if you want the salad to be a little spicy, shake over some hot paprika.

(Continued)

For the vegetables, boil the potatoes, halved, in salted water for 8 to 10 minutes, until knife tender. Halve and peel the onion. Quarter it, then pull the layers apart, making a pile of onion petals. Let the onions cook gently for a while until they start to soften and color on one side. Then carefully flip them and cook the other sides. When they are perfectly semi-caramelized, they're done and can be set aside. Heat the same cast-iron pan to medium-high, add another glug of oil, and fry the potatoes on both sides until browned and crisp.

Tear or cut the kale leaves from the stalks, roll them up into a cigar shape, then slice into strips. In a large bowl, squeeze over some lemon juice, scatter a pinch of flaky salt, and then squeeze the kale leaves until the color brightens and they tenderize a bit.

Slice the carrots into thin pieces, leaving some a bit long, then dress with tarragon white wine vinegar and a little flaky salt.

Thinly slice the persimmon and pear half, then cut down to your desired bite size. Squeeze lemon juice over both and set aside.

Brush all the dirt off of the mushrooms and break them into 1-inch pieces. Heat a skillet with a lid over medium heat and add 2 tablespoons butter. When it starts to melt, add the mushrooms, tossing to coat, then cover the pan and reduce the heat to medium-low. Cook for about 5 minutes this way, lifting the lid once to check that they aren't burning and that the steam is making them properly tender. Flip the mushrooms over, cover the pan again, and reduce the heat to low or remove from the heat entirely, depending on how soon you will eat. Lobster mushrooms require this steaming in the pan to properly tenderize and reach their greatest flavor potential.

To make the dressing, combine the tahini, 2 tablespoons olive oil, 1 table-spoon lemon juice, a little salt, and your desired seasonings, then whisk actively with a fork. It may clump up; if so, add water, a drizzle at a time, and keep going with the fork until you have a smooth dressing of whatever thick-ness you desire.

To assemble the salads, place a generous handful of the kale leaves on each plate or bowl. Tuck the potatoes all around. Lay over the onion petals. Scatter over some of the crispy rice. Add a small handful of more kale. Tuck the car-rots in all around. Scatter over more of the crispy rice. Lay slices of persimmon and pear gently all around. Top with the still-warm mushrooms from the pan. Another scattering of crispy rice. Pass around a cup of the tahini dressing at the table. Have fun splattering your salad like a Jackson Pollock painting.

squash and mushroom rye galette, with goat cheese and fried shallots

My mom made the savory pies from the *Moosewood Cookbook* and *The Enchanted Broccoli Forest* for my late-teen birthdays and other special occasions around that time. My college roommates would also make them for me, on the opening nights of plays or on my birthday or whatever. It was the primary dish that could put an ear-to-ear grin on my face. In my adult life I've made them often, but probably not often enough. Nothing is more nostalgic and comforting to me. This fall version has a particularly nice seasonal flavor profile, but consider it a jumping off point for whatever flavors suit your fancy.

Rye crust:

1 stick (113 grams) unsalted butter

1 cup (125 grams) all-purpose flour

Heaping ½ cup dark northern rye flour

½ teaspoon salt

5 to 8 teaspoons ice water

Squash and mushroom filling:

1 red kuri or sweetmeat squash

Butter

Olive oil

1 bulb of garlic

Salt

1 medium or 2 small shallots

Chèvre

½ pound (or just slightly less) wild or cultivated mushrooms

Hungarian paprika

Flaky salt

For the rye crust, cut and crumble the butter into small pieces, then freeze it. After 20 minutes or so, place the flours, salt, and butter into a food processor and blitz. Many quality pie recipes expound on the fine pleasures of rubbing the butter in with your hands. I agree, but it is easier to get perfect, flaky crust by forming pebbles of cold butter, and this is much more achievable in the food processor. After blitzing for 30 seconds or so, stop, check, then pulse. Add 2 teaspoons of water, pulse again and move to another bowl. Add more ice water, 1 teaspoon at a time, mixing with a wooden spoon until the dough balls up. Roll the dough ball in flour, wrap in plastic wrap, then place in the fridge for 45 to 60 minutes (or freeze until you want to make the galette).

For the filling, cut the skin off the squash, cut it in half, scoop out the seeds and pulp, then cut it into strips about 2½ inches long. Toss the pieces with a mixture of melted butter and olive oil. Cut the top off of the bulb of garlic, peeling the excess papery skin off too. Drizzle with olive oil, sprinkle with salt

(*Continued*)

and set in the center of the squash. Bake at 400 degrees F for 30 to 45 minutes, moving the pieces of squash around in the oil, scraping off the bottom of the pan and adjusting its placement in the oven every 10 minutes or so. When the squash is tender and has begun to darken in color, take it out. If the roasted garlic isn't quite there yet, remove it to another pan and cook for an additional 10 to 15 minutes, or until soft, spreadable, and meltingly tender.

Midway through this process, take the ball of dough out of the fridge and roll it out into a rough circle slightly wider than your baking pan. Place this in the freezer to firm up.

Slice the shallot thinly, then chop the thin slices aggressively. Coat the bottom of a thin pan with oil. Heat on high until the oil shimmers, then drop in the shallot pieces. Add salt. Leave for approximately 1 minute, then agitate. When they've started to crisp up, turn off the heat. The shallots will finish cooking in the hot oil. Leave them for just a few minutes. Drain and remove to a bowl, ready to be sprinkled on at the end.

Break apart the little ball of chèvre (the kind that comes rolled in paprika is great for this) into little pieces. Place in a bowl, at the ready.

Lay the frozen, open galette dough on a work surface. Spread the roasted garlic in a circle in the center like a pizza sauce. Set the squash pieces on top of the roasted garlic spread, and fold the edges of the pastry over. Bake at 425 degrees F for 10 minutes, then at 375 degrees F for 20 minutes, then at 325 degrees F for 10 to 15 more minutes to finish. By the time you're down to 325 degrees F it will be all cooked and ready. You're just waiting for the crust to brown slightly and flake to perfection.

During the last 10 minutes the galette is in the oven: heat some more butter and oil in the pan that recently held the shallots. Break the mushrooms apart into your preferred size. When the oil is hot, add them to the pan. Cover with a lid for 1 minute. Remove the lid and agitate the mushrooms. They'll be tender and too moist; now you're cooking the excess moisture out of them. Press down on them with a spatula. Hear the water sizzle out. The pan-side edges should start to turn appetizingly brown. Flip those mushrooms over to do the other side. When all are pretty much done, turn down to low and hold until the galette is finished.

When the galette is ready, pull it out and drop the chèvre pieces evenly over the squash. Scatter the mushroom pieces on top, then sprinkle with the crispy shallots. Sprinkle the Hungarian paprika over the pieces of chèvre and add a light dusting of flaky salt on the sweeter, squash-heavy areas. Serve hot, with a bowl of soup and/or an autumnal salad with some crunch. The galette is also delicious at room temperature. Take a slice for lunch the next day and follow it with a pear and a handful of nuts.

SNAPSHOTS OF EATING AND COOKING

In college, I am living with fourteen people in a co-op house in a historic Vermont village. When I cook with Amy, who is also from Oregon, we're known as "Oregon Trail." Some Tuesday, we are looking out over the scene we have created: a sea of wool sweaters, plates on laps, smiling faces, autumnal vegetables spilling out of every dish, and more dressings and dips than we can count. We've produced food that feels like how the Moosewood Restaurant must have been when it first opened. A quiet high five in the hallway, as someone flips the record.

RISOTTOS

Some general notes on tools and techniques for risotto:

I feel strongly that a pan with a wide base is essential for making good risotto.

A good stirring/scraping tool is also essential. Make sure your tool can safely scrape the bottom of your pan. A wooden flat spatula (just make sure the tip is thin enough) is good on enamel pots, a strong metal spatula is best on steel.

I'm an onion-sensitive cook. It's a downfall, and sometimes I don't want to wear my goggles. The one time I find the usually undesirable qualities of a food-processed onion to be good is when making risotto. The onions are smashed, wet, and ready to disappear into the butter, oil, rice, and broth.

On the process of cooking the risotto:

After the allium is softened and the rice has had a minute to fry and absorb some fat, make a circle with your tool. Pour in the wine and scrape it all around evenly, deglazing the pan and impregnating the rice with the alcohol. Let that cook for a minute or two, until the wine has all been absorbed, then make another circle with your tool. Add a ladleful of stock, then stir vigorously to incorporate. Repeat this process, taking progressively longer between ladlefuls. You'll notice the stock absorbs quite quickly at first, then as the rice cooks, it will slow. You don't want the rice to break down very much and become gummy, so the sweet spot is where you can feel whole grains on your tongue but they are entirely tender.

leek risotto with blue cheese and hazelnut oil

In the winter, the prospect of making a leek risotto can really brighten the evening. Head home in the early darkness, and enjoy watching the heat in the kitchen react with the frosted window-panes. In this one, the blue cheese provides the deep savor, and the hazelnut oil rounds it out perfectly.

---

2 quarts good vegetable stock

5 tablespoons cold butter

2 tablespoons olive oil

1 leek

1¾ cup arborio rice

About 1 cup white wine

¼ cup grated Parmesan

Salt

About ½ of a cake-slice wedge of blue cheese (Point Reyes highly recommended)

2 teaspoons hazelnut or walnut oil

Warm the stock in a medium soup pot over medium-low heat.

In a half-height soup pot or Dutch oven, melt 3 tablespoons of the butter into the olive oil over medium-low heat while slicing, then chopping the leek. Reserve the tops. Add the chopped leeks to the pot and stir to coat. Cook over medium heat for about 2 minutes, or until the pieces soften.

Add the arborio rice to the pot with the leek, stir, and cook for another 2 minutes. Turn up the heat, and when things start to sizzle, pour in the wine for a good "wow" moment. Stir vigorously and return the heat to medium. Once the wine has absorbed, start adding the stock, one ladleful at a time, waiting until all the stock has absorbed before adding the next ladleful.

About 20 minutes later, the rice should be luscious but still have a bit of bite. It should stick to the spoon. When this "Is my oatmeal done? Yes, I think so," moment has happened, turn off the heat.

Slice and stir in the remaining 2 tablespoons cold butter. Stir in the Parmesan. Salt to taste, then add the blue cheese, to taste. At long last, add the nut oil— about 2 teaspoons, but also to taste.

Slice the leek tops into ¼-inch strips, then split the strips at the tips and pull them apart. Heat a dry cast-iron pan and lay the curly strips in the pan. When they've crisped up a bit and just started to color, take them off and use them to top each serving of risotto.

spring risotto with trout and green garlic

This is my absolute favorite way to prepare a whole fish. The texture is perfectly silky and ideal for flaking into risotto. The same method can be applied to other fish. The only thing that should be adjusted is the time in the oven, based on the size of the fish.

Try making this one on a rainy night, sipping a Venetian-style Campari or Aperol spritzer, and serve it with a salad of simply dressed spring greens.

---

1 whole dressed trout	A few stalks of green garlic
2 or 3 lime leaves	5 tablespoons cold butter
Olive oil	1¾ cups arborio rice
Flaky salt	About 1 cup white wine
2 quarts fish stock	¼ cup grated Pecorino Romano
1 white onion	

If you have the time, you can bake the trout in advance and use the trout skeleton and head to make a fish stock, but you'll likely need some other pieces of fish. To make good fish stock, use a healthy combination of skeleton, heads, and skins. Add a cheesecloth bundle of fresh herbs. Simmer for 1 to 2 hours over medium-low heat. Salt cautiously to taste.

To prepare the trout, wash the fish under cold running water. Check the insides for stray guts and, if you see any, get rid of them! Place the lime leaves in the cavity of the fish. Drizzle a little olive oil over the skin, and sprinkle on a little flaky salt. Set the fish on a rectangle of parchment paper, then twist up the ends like a candy wrapper.

Bake the trout at 375 degrees F for 15 to 20 minutes (this will be longer for fish larger than trout). Check after 12 minutes or so, just to be sure. There is a fine line between done and underdone whole fish! The flesh should be opaque but so, so tender. Remove the fish, let it cool, then split it open and pull away the skeleton. It should come out just fine. Cut the head off, flip the whole trout over, and gently peel off the skin. Reserve it for trout bacon or a fish stock. There may be some grey membrane between the flesh and the skin. It is delicious, just not very attractive. Scrape this off gently with a spoon (eat it, stir it into the finished risotto, or drop it in the stock, whatever you feel like). You'll be left with stunning pieces of flaky trout.

For the risotto, warm the fish stock in a medium soup pot over medium-low heat.

Peel and slice the onion, then chop it very finely. Trim and chop the green garlic, saving about one-quarter of it for later. Melt 3 tablespoons of the butter into the olive oil in your good-for-risotto soup pot, then add the onion and green garlic.

Cook over medium heat until the onion is translucent and the green garlic has gotten quite soft. Add the arborio rice, stir to incorporate, and cook for about 2 minutes. Scrape a hole in the center, add the wine, watch it sizzle, then stir vigorously.

After another couple of minutes, when the rice is just starting to stick a little, scrape another hole in the center and add a ladleful of stock. Repeat until the rice is perfect, about 20 minutes or so, waiting until all the stock has absorbed before adding the next ladleful.

Turn off the heat, then stir in most of the grated pecorino and remaining 2 tablespoons cold butter. Cook the reserved green garlic in a small frying pan in butter. Flake apart the fish, then stir it into the risotto a few pieces at a time. Reserve a few pieces to put on top of the individual servings, along with the sautéed green garlic.

squash blossom and young garlic risotto

At the height of summer, from the farmers' market or your own garden, celebrate the gorgeous young garlic and squash blossoms with this risotto! Eat it outside, with rosé, because you deserve it.

---

2 quarts vegetable or chicken stock

4 or 5 cloves mild, young garlic with soft, wet skins

1 large or 2 smaller spring onions

Several squash blossoms

5 tablespoons cold butter, divided

Olive oil

1¾ cups arborio rice

About 1 cup white wine

¼ cup grated Parmesan, plus more for serving

Warm your stock in a medium soup pot over medium-low heat.

Peel, slice, and chop the garlic and spring onions. Wash and set aside your squash blossoms.

Melt the 3 tablespoons of the butter and olive oil in your soup pot or Dutch oven. Add the onions and garlic and cook over medium heat until softened. Add the arborio rice and cook for a minute or two more. Scrape out a circle in the center, then add the white wine. It should sizzle and steam on contact. Stir vigorously so the rice absorbs the alcohol. Cook this way for about 2 minutes, or until the liquid is gone and the rice is just barely starting to stick to the bottom of the pan.

Scape out another circle, add a ladleful of stock, stir vigorously to incorporate, and repeat this process, remembering to take just a bit longer between ladlefuls as the stock is absorbed.

When most of the stock is absorbed (I almost always stop before I've reached the end of the pot) and the risotto is delicious, turn the heat off. Add the squash blossoms, Parmesan, and remaining 2 tablespoons butter. Stir to incorporate, then cover to let the squash blossoms delicately steam.

This risotto goes quite well with grilled summer vegetables. Top each serving with another sprinkling of Parmesan.

You could also make a fresh young garlic stock by cooking some other cloves in butter, topping off with salt and water, then boiling/simmering (perhaps with a cheesecloth sachet or other good stock items) until the taste comes through.

hedgehog mushroom risotto

If you can get your hands on hedgehog mushrooms, they add a lemony, chickeny quality that is really perfect in this setting. In the fall, I love to make a batch of mushroom risotto and a salad like the kale Caesar in *Tartine Bread*, pour glasses of dry white table wine, leave the hunk of Parmesan on the table, and listen to the wacky local independent radio station.

---

2 quarts vegetable or mushroom stock	1¾ cups arborio rice
1 onion	Hedgehog or other similar wild mushrooms
5 tablespoons cold butter, divided	Parmesan
About 1 cup dry white wine	

Brush and tear apart the wild mushrooms and set them aside, all ready to be cooked while stirring the risotto.

Warm your stock in a medium soup pot over medium-low heat.

Peel, slice, and finely chop the onion, or blitz in a food processor. Melt 3 tablespoons of the butter in your good soup pot or Dutch oven. Add the onion and cook on medium-high until it gets translucent and then just starts to color. Add just a splash of wine (there'll be a fun explosion of steam) and all the arborio rice. Stir and cook for about 1 minute.

Using a metal spatula rather than a wooden spoon (if your good pot is made of something that can handle this), scrape the rice and onion away to the edges, leaving a circle in the center. Pour in the rest of the wine in a slow stream, stirring to incorporate.

When the alcohol has evaporated, add the first ladleful of hot stock. Stir to absorb, add more stock, and repeat. You'll be at the stove doing this for about 20 minutes.

Cook the wild mushrooms simply in a mixture of butter and olive oil over medium heat. If you can handle the multitasking, this can be done at the same time as the ladling and stirring of the risotto. Hedgehogs are mushrooms that I don't fuss over getting to be dry and crispy; they have a sort of tangy, stewed-meat quality to them. For this, try cooking them until they start to go dry, and then add a ladleful of stock to the mushroom pan. Tip that in with the risotto when you are nearly through adding the stock, perhaps saving a few mushrooms to top each serving.

When the stock has all been absorbed, add the remaining 2 tablespoons cold butter and a handful of Parmesan. Cover the pan and turn off the burner.

Serve in medium, shallow bowls with a road of Parmesan down the middle. This is really very good with cold crunchy simple salads, like one of fennel and mint.

I like to use a mushroom-leaning vegetable stock when making something like this. For this dish on the day we shot the photo, I used a roasted garlic stock from the freezer and amended it with mushroom paste and some water from rehydrated dried porcinis. Make sure the stock has the amount of saltiness you want in your finished risotto. Risotto's beautiful creamy texture is disrupted by extra seasonings, so try to nail the stock first; that's kind of the whole idea!

PIZZAS

pizza dough, white and wheat

These are my two go-to pizza dough formulas. I encourage you to try them both. They are intentionally somewhere between the long-fermented, complicated recipes found in the great pizza books and the "how do I get this pizza on the table?" internet recipes.

I have bricks in the base of my oven, and have found over time that both the easiest and most consistent results come from heating the oven to 550 degrees F and baking the pizzas on thin baking sheets, directly on top of the bricks. You can use a fancy pizza stone, but don't really need the stone element to make great pizza. The idea is to figure out what works best for your own oven.

Each recipe makes enough dough for two rectangular pizzas made on standard baking sheets. This dough can be made the night before or the morning of the day that the pizza will be eaten.

Traditional pizza dough:

¼ teaspoon (1 gram) instant dry yeast

1½ cups (350 grams) warm water

1 messy tablespoon (approximately 20 grams) sourdough starter, if you have one

4 cups (500 grams) all-purpose flour

1½ teaspoons (10 grams) fine sea salt

Whole wheat pizza dough:

¼ teaspoon (1 gram) instant dry yeast

1¾ cups (400 grams) warm water (whole wheat flour absorbs more water, so a higher rate of hydration is necessary)

1 messy tablespoon (approximately 20 grams) sourdough starter, if you have one

3 cups (350 grams) all-purpose flour

1 cup (150 grams) whole wheat flour

1 tablespoon (20 grams) fine sea salt (whole wheat crust tends to turn out sweeter, so I have a much larger quantity of salt here)

Mix the yeast with the warm water, add the sourdough starter, and leave it to proof for 10 minutes. Little bubbles should appear on the surface. Using this technique of combing dry and wild yeast (I keep a bread starter active and use it often for things like this), you should definitely get some bubbles.

In a good mixing bowl, prepare the flour: make a well in the center and add about half of the yeast mixture, stirring to incorporate. Add the second half, continuing to mix, then add the salt and mix it in with your hands.

Let the dough rest for about 30 minutes, giving the gluten time to do its thing. Then knead the dough actively for 10 to 15 minutes, either with a stand mixer's bread hook or with your knuckles, fists, and wrists. Cover the mixing bowl with plastic wrap, a garbage bag, or a plastic grocery bag and leave it in the fridge to bulk ferment slowly. I've had equally good results making it the night before, the morning of an evening pizza dinner, and even within a couple of hours. But if you only have a couple of hours, skip the fridge and ferment it in a warm place. When you are getting ready to bake, take out the dough and let it rise sitting on the stovetop, while the oven creeps up to its maximum heat.

potato, manchego, oregano pizza

I admit it, this recipe started with fancying the assonance when it first popped into my mind. I was on the playground at school one miserably cold winter day, thinking about how sparse my fridge was but knowing I didn't even want to stop on the way home for ingredients. I had some Manchego left over from some other dinner and about three potatoes. Wild oregano grows rampant in my backyard garden. I remember my roommates having a bunch of friends over for takeout that night, all of them laughing and eating in the living room while I waited for the dough to rise for my tan pizza. But it was a damn good tan pizza.

When we shot the dish for this book, I had prepared salt cod (quite optional) in the freezer, left over from a Secret Restaurant dinner, and it took the dish from the "cheap, easy, weeknight" zone into the "special, to be had with good wine" zone.

---

2 Yukon Gold potatoes	Cream Sauce (recipe follows)
Manchego cheese	Flaky salt
A softer mild cheese (something else from Spain, or a local farmstead cheese)	Salt cod (optional) (This is a great use for leftover salt cod. Or, process the salt cod to have dollops on your pizza, and the next day make salt cod fritters or another favorite salt cod dish.)
Fresh or dried oregano	
Whole Wheat Pizza Dough (page 132)	

Bring a saucepan of generously salted water to a boil. Slice the very well-scrubbed Yukon Gold potatoes. Using a spider spoon or whatever you have for such an operation, transfer the potatoes to the boiling water. Cook for approximately 5 minutes. You want them to be just shy of done, so they shouldn't fall apart when a fork pricks them, but they also shouldn't push back.

While the potatoes cook, grate and slice your Manchego and other Spanish cheese.

When the potatoes are done, lift or strain them out and set aside. Strip the fresh oregano from its stalks. If the leaves are tiny, don't bother chopping them. If they are pretty big, chop roughly. If you don't live somewhere where oregano grows all year long, or don't otherwise have access to fresh oregano, using dried is fine, just use a lot—a healthy sprinkling over the first layer of sauce would be a good idea.

Toss the pizza dough and stretch to fit a baking sheet. Spread the dough with the cream sauce and sprinkle with oregano, then layer the potatoes and top with flaky salt and more oregano. Sprinkle on the Manchego and even more oregano. Arrange the softer cheese and salt cod on top.

Bake between 500 degrees F and 550 degrees F, or the best your oven can do, for anywhere from 5 to 15 minutes. Remove when the edges are golden and the cheese is browning in places.

CREAM SAUCE

2 or 3 cloves garlic

2 tablespoons butter

1 tablespoon all-purpose flour

About 1½ cups heavy cream

White pepper

Salt (truffle salt, if you have it)

Green garlic powder (if you have it or can make it)

Onion powder

Mince the garlic and put it in a small saucepan with the butter. Cook the garlic until fragrant. Add the flour, then whisk it swiftly, cooking for a few moments until the mixture smells biscuity. Slowly add some cream, whisking to incorporate. When the sauce is smooth and starts to thicken, add more of the cream and repeat. Add the white pepper, salt, green garlic powder, and onion powder. Turn the heat down to low, then stir actively for 5 to 10 minutes, or until the cream sauce is garlicky, a little spicy, and delicious.

porchini, garlic scape, and sea bean white pizza

I feel quite proud of this pizza. The garlic scapes roast as the pizza bakes, and their aromatics infuse the whole pie. The porcini delicately flavors the blissfully melting cheese, and the sea beans lift every other bite with their salty, fresh crunch.

Traditional Pizza Dough (page 132)

Cream Sauce (page 137)

Mozzarella

Garlic scapes

Franklin's Teleme cheese (from San Luis Obispo, CA) (you could also just ask the person at your cheese counter if they have Franklin's Teleme, and if they don't, what a good substitution would be. Often there are other fresh jack cheeses that work very similarly. Beecher's makes a great one.)

1 porcini mushroom (or 2, but it'll cost like $3.50 for one!)

Wild sea beans (common in Oregon, maybe less common other places; substitute capers if you can't find them)

Toss the pizza dough and stretch to fit a baking sheet. Spread the dough with the cream sauce, add the mozzarella, then arrange the garlic scapes. Arrange the cheese all over. Thinly slice or shave the porcini, then arrange evenly around the pizza.

Bake between 500 degrees F and 550 degrees F, or the best your oven can do, for anywhere from 5 to 15 minutes. When the pizza is bubbling hot and slightly golden around the edges, take it out and add the sea beans to the top.

zucchini, anchovy, tomato pizza with calabrian chilies and basil oil

A high-summer, maximalist pizza. I decided to just go for it and bring every one of my favorite elements of traditional Italian pizzas into one. I knew there was a risk of a dysfunctional Olympic team situation, where all the great players might not get along, but found it suited them to join up together. The Calabrian chilies spice up the tomato sauce and brighten the melted mozzarella, the zucchini and fresh tomato provide balance and substance, the anchovies and basil oil blast the taste buds every few bites, and the goat cheese surprises and evens everything out with its creamy texture and piquant flavor.

Basil oil:

1 stalk basil, abundant with leaves

1 clove garlic

½ cup olive oil

Good red sauce:

2 to 3 cloves of garlic

Salt

1 shallot

Olive oil

1 can good diced tomatoes

Balsamic or red wine vinegar

Black pepper

Red pepper flakes

6 small oil-packed or 2 larger salt-packed anchovies, cut into 6 strips

3 or 4 Calabrian chilies

1 small green zucchini

1 tomato

Traditional Pizza Dough (page 132)

Mozzarella

Leonora goat cheese (this is a fancy, exquisite goat cheese; you can substitute a less fancy brand/style to no detriment)

Parmesan

Olive oil

To make the basil oil, place the blade and bowl of your food processor in the freezer. De-stem the basil. Peel the clove of garlic. Heat the olive oil in a tiny saucepan. When you can feel the heat radiating when you place your hand over the pan, it's ready. Place the basil leaves and garlic into the oil, turn the heat down to low, and simmer for 5 to 10 minutes. When it seems like the basil is just starting to cook and lose its color, that's when it's done. Turn off the heat and leave the oil to cool completely. When it is cool, remove the garlic clove. Take the food processor parts out of the freezer, pour the oil and basil in, pulse a few times, then blitz—it should take less than 30 seconds. The oil might go creamy here, but that's okay! It'll settle. You'll be left with a very delicious green oil.

(Continued)

For a good quick red sauce, peel the garlic cloves and place them in a mortar and pestle. Sprinkle with salt, glug in some olive oil. Smash the cloves into a rough paste with the pestle. Peel and mince the shallot. Add this to the smashed garlic with a little more oil and salt, doing your best to bring them together smoothly.

Heat some olive oil in a small saucepan, then add the mixture of shallot and garlic. Cook until fragrant—a few minutes. Add the canned tomatoes, stirring to mix the garlic and shallot. Add a splash of balsamic vinegar, a cracking of black pepper and a pinch of red pepper flakes. Raise the heat until the sauce starts to bubble, then reduce to a simmer. Let it cook, with an occasional stir, for the duration of your pizza prep time. Continue to taste it, adding more vinegar (or the red wine you might be drinking), salt, pepper, or red pepper flakes as desired. About halfway through cooking, or really whenever you have a free moment, blend it a little with an immersion blender. This step is only for texture, so if you don't have one, it is quite all right.

To prep the toppings, chop the oil-packed anchovies or, if using salt-packed, wash the salt off and let them soak for a few minutes in warm water, then pull out the skeletons and cut into your desired size. Chop the Calabrian chilies, scooping out the seeds as you go. Cut the zucchini into long strips with a vegetable peeler. Slice the tomato thinly.

Toss the pizza dough and stretch to fit a baking sheet. Spread the sauce, arrange the chilies, and sprinkle with mozzarella. Arrange the zucchini strips, brushing them with olive oil, and then arrange the tomatoes slices and anchovies. Dot with the goat cheese. Sprinkle with some Parmesan.

Bake between 500 degrees F and 550 degrees F, or the best your oven can do, for anywhere from 5 to 15 minutes, until the cheese has melted and the crust has browned around the edges. When it is cooling, drizzle basil oil on all the right spots.

mushroom pizza with roasted garlic-squash sauce, candied tomatoes, and arugula

The first year I lived in my apartment, we did a Secret Restaurant pizza night. The idea was sparked because my roommates had moved out and taken the dining room table with them. We planned to build a new one ourselves but didn't have the time just yet, so we wanted to do a dinner that didn't require a table. We made so much pizza, the guests actually had to tell us to stop. "No more!" they cried, when we were about two-thirds of the way through our planned pies. The dinner was in the fall, and I made this great roasted garlic-squash sauce. Only three of the six pizzas intended to have the squash sauce were made, so the next night a few of us got together and had chanterelle and squash sauce calzones.

When coming up with this pizza, specifically, there were four influences: the memory of the squash sauce on pizza night, the quantity of mushrooms on the mushroom pie at Delancey in Seattle, the candied tomatoes Sofie so successfully wooed me with many moons ago, and the wild arugula growing rampant in my backyard.

Sauce:

1 small winter squash

Olive oil

Salt

1 small eggplant

1 bulb of garlic

Lots of cremini mushrooms (a pound, at least)

Butter

Candied Tomatoes (page 186) or sundried tomatoes

Good aged pecorino

Whole Wheat Pizza Dough (page 132)

Mozzarella

Red pepper flakes (optional)

Arugula

To make the squash sauce, set the oven to 375 degrees F. Chop the winter squash in half, then in quarters. Scoop out the seeds and guts and wash under

(Continued)

running water. This will get any dirt off the skin and provide some extra moisture to steam the flesh. Brush with olive oil and dust with salt.

Wash and trim the end off the eggplant and cut in half. Score the flesh, brush with olive oil and dust with salt. Cut the garlic bulb down the middle and break in two. Use the half that has exposed cloves, trimming the top off as well.

Arrange the squash and eggplant pieces around the garlic in a roasting tin. Pour olive oil onto the exposed top of the garlic, then sprinkle with salt. Roast for about 1 hour, or until all three are soft and cooked through.

Pull the squash and eggplant flesh out of their respective skins. Pop the garlic cloves out of their skins too. Discard all of these skins. Combine the cooked vegetables in a tall saucepan or jar, then use an immersion blender to puree them all together. If you don't have an immersion blender, the same result can be achieved with a food processor or a vigorous hand and fork.

The flavor should be exquisite as is, but if it is missing anything, try apple cider vinegar (for brightness), cayenne or red pepper flakes (if you want it a little spicy), or simply some more salt.

Slice the mushrooms and sauté them in a mixture of olive oil and butter until they are a warm, woody brown. Do this in batches until you have a nice heaping pile of mushrooms. Set aside.

Set out (or defrost) your jar of candied tomatoes, or soak some sun-dried tomatoes in olive oil and add a splash of red wine vinegar.

Make some larger rectangular shavings of aged pecorino for the top of the finished pizza and grate some to mix with the mozzarella for cooking. Toss the pizza dough and stretch to fit a baking sheet. Spread the sauce, then sprinkle the mozzarella and grated pecorino. Arrange the mushrooms and tomatoes and top with a little more grated pecorino.

Bake between 500 degrees F and 550 degrees F, or the best your oven can do, for 10 to 15 minutes. When it is done, let it sit for about 3 minutes, then add the large shavings of pecorino and a scant dusting of red pepper flakes, if you like them. Wash and dry the arugula, adding it raw to the top of the smoking hot pizza.

PANZANELLAS

shallots braised with tamarind, lacinato kale, and purple potato panzanella

The braised shallots in this salad were inspired by a small plate at a favorite restaurant. I left wanting to eat more of the shallots with more of the bread. The best thing to do was figure out how to make them myself, and to create a new dish using the favorite part (bread in sauce) as the focus.

Purple potatoes	Shallots
Olive oil	Tamarind paste
Salt	Lacinato kale
Day-old crusty, naturally leavened sourdough bread	Lemon juice
	Black pepper

Slice the purple potatoes into quarters or smaller, place them in a roasting tin, drizzle with olive oil, sprinkle with plenty of salt, and toss to coat. Roast at 425 degrees F for 30 to 40 minutes, or until they start to crisp around the edges.

Slice and tear the bread into bite-size pieces. If your bread isn't old, throw it on a baking sheet and into the oven at 425 degrees F for about 5 minutes.

Peel the shallots and slice them in half lengthwise. Coat the bottom of a deep-rimmed, pan with a lid or Dutch oven with olive oil. Add the shallots, some salt and 1 teaspoon tamarind paste. Stir the tamarind—as it heats it should melt into the olive oil. Cook, covered, over medium heat. The moisture should cause the shallots to sweat into the tamarind oil quite quickly. Remove the lid and check on them after about 10 minutes. Press into them with your spatula to get the pieces separated. Cover again, lower the heat to medium low, and continue cooking until the shallots have that melt-in-your-mouth quality.

Strip the lacinato kale from its stalks, roll up the leaves, and cut into ¼-inch slices. This will result in lots of thin strips. Add some lemon juice and salt, toss to coat, then squeeze the strips to encourage the acid to tenderize them.

When the potatoes are done, toss them with the bread. Then add the shallots, even using some of the bread to wipe up every last drop of sauce from the cooking pan. Add the kale strips. Season with some black pepper, toss again, and serve.

niçoise panzanella

This dish should be a contender for your first picnic of the year!
Keep it simple and have this panzanella in a park or on a mountain,
with a dry white, a rosé, or a good pilsner, and nothing else.

White crusty loaf

1 can good, fatty wild pink salmon from
the Northwest or Scotland or cold salmon
leftover from another dinner

Flaky salt

Lemons

Castelvetrano olives

Olive oil

Curly endive, frisée, or escarole

Flat-leaf parsley

A few sorrel leaves, if you can get them

Black pepper

Cut the bread into slices, then into bite-size pieces. Tear some of these pieces
in half with your hands. If the bread is really stale, sprinkle with water and
toast in the oven to bring it back to life a bit. If it is new but not super flavorful, drizzle some olive oil or throw some white wine vinegar at it.

Drain the salmon, turn it out into a mixing bowl. Sprinkle with flaky salt and
a squeeze of lemon juice.

Pit and chop or tear the olives. Add to the salmon and mix without ceremony.
Taste. If the salmon is fatty enough you might not need it, but maybe add
some olive oil.

Wash and dry the greens. Chop off the bigger bottom stem of the parsley, and
then roughly chop the remainder. Mix with the other greens. Dress with a
squeeze of lemon juice, more flaky salt, and a little olive oil.

Slice a lemon into discs, then cut around the edges to remove the peel,
sectioning off little triangles of flesh.

Combine the salmon mixture with the bread pieces and toss lightly. Season
with a very generous amount of black pepper. Then add the dressed greens
and toss lightly again. Add the lemon flesh to the bowl or divide it into the
individual servings.

classic italian summer panzanella

This transcendent meal can be made from a little high-summer produce and some old bread.

---

1 very small or ½ large fresh sweet onion

4 or so cloves garlic

White wine vinegar

Lemon juice

Olive oil

Salt

7 to 12 ripe tomatoes (several kinds if you can buy or grow them)

Cucumber

Pickled green peppercorns (this is the secret, important ingredient here; find them at specialty food markets, or online;

Napoleon, a very common brand, makes them)

Parmesan

Fresh mozzarella

Basil, parsley, celery leaves, or whatever strong leafy herb you have available

The best damn stale bread you can get (2 to 3 handfuls of crouton-size pieces)

Red wine (already open, just for cooking or what you are drinking that night)

Black pepper

Dice the onion finely and place it in a nonreactive bowl (a glass mixing bowl is perfect). Peel and mince the garlic, adding it to the onion. Pour in enough white wine vinegar to soak them both. Add lemon juice until they are almost submerged. Add olive oil to really bury them. Salt generously. Let this hang out for at least 1 hour—seriously. You can get away with 30 minutes but an hour is better. This is the technique that gives this panzanella its brightness, its zing.

If you are cooking other food, work on it now, or take a walk, or read a chapter of your book.

Wash, de-stem, and slice the tomatoes. If you have cherry tomatoes, simply slice them in half. Other tomatoes? Medium slices, with a couple rough chops to break them up. If using an English cucumber, no need to fuss over it. A regular one? Peel a couple lines down the outer skin and scoop out the seeds before cutting it into half-moon slices. Little lemon cucumbers? Wash the prickles off, but no need to de-seed. Smash and chop about 1 teaspoon pickled green peppercorns. Add them with the tomatoes and cucumbers to the onion mixture.

During the 10 minutes or so it takes for these things to become acquainted, grate the Parmesan, tear the mozzarella, and tear the herbs. Add the bread pieces to the rest of the salad. Toss aggressively, splashing in red wine as you go. Try to get the wine to hit half the bread pieces. Toss in the Parmesan, mozzarella, and herbs. Drizzle with olive oil, taste, and add more wine, wine vinegar, lemon juice, salt, or black pepper to taste.

squash, mustard green, and pickled mushroom panzanella

The squash is sweet and satisfying, the mustard greens healthful and spicy, and the pickled mushrooms carry through the early note while also being light and tangy.

This is the kind of dish you could eat a large serving bowl's worth of and want to do it again the next day.

Apple cider vinegar	1 good winter squash
White wine vinegar	Olive oil
Ginger, peeled and sliced	Flaky salt
Garlic, peeled	Good rustic wheat bread
Button or cremini mushrooms	Mustard greens

Pickle the mushrooms ahead of time: heat the apple cider vinegar, white wine vinegar, ginger, and garlic in a small saucepan. Slice your mushrooms as thinly as possible. Tuck them into a jar. Pour the hot vinegar over them, seal the lid, refrigerate, and wait a few days.

Prepare your winter squash by cutting it in half, scooping the seeds out, scraping the inside smooth, and then peeling the skin off. Cut long pieces about ½ inch thick, then cut each one into three or four smaller pieces. Dress with olive oil, flaky salt, and a little apple cider vinegar. Roast in the oven at 425 degrees F until the squash starts to darken and some edges have caramelized. Take them out and move them around a few times during the roasting so they color evenly and don't overcook on the bottoms.

While the squash roasts, slice, tear, and toast the bread. Wash and dry the mustard greens, chopping or tearing them to make a nice tall pile on the cutting board. Heat some oil in a wok or other large pan, add the greens with a sprinkling of salt and a little white wine vinegar, then turn over quickly until wilted.

Combine the bread, mustard greens, squash slices, and pickled mushrooms. Drizzle with olive oil, toss, then drizzle with olive oil again. Season with flaky salt. Taste, adjust, devour.

PASTAS

black pepper pasta with aged pecorino and oregano

This simple dish is all about celebrating the extra goodness of homemade pasta and strong flavors in balance.

Black pepper pasta (per portion):

1 cup all-purpose flour

1 egg per cup of flour

A pinch of salt

1 tablespoon powdered porcini mushrooms (if you can find it!) per 1 to 3 portions

Lots of black pepper—so much you can actually see it

A few teaspoons water, if necessary

Fresh oregano

Aged pecorino

A knob of butter

For the pasta, portion the flour into a mixing bowl, making a well in the center. Crack the egg(s) into the well and beat with a fork. Start to fork in the flour, pausing to add the pinch of salt, the mushroom powder, black pepper, and a little water if it still seems too dry. Knead the dough for 10 minutes, using your hands or the dough hook of a stand mixer.

When dough is "smooth as a baby's bottom," cover it in plastic wrap and place it in the fridge. Let it rest for at least 30 minutes. Flatten it into a square, and section off into rectangles with a dough scraper. Press the sections flat (a grill spatula works great for this). Roll the dough out into increasingly thinner sections with a stand mixer pasta attachment or hand-crank pasta machine, then cut into fettuccine.

Boil some water and add a dash of salt. Strip the fresh oregano from its stalks and chop roughly. Grate the aged pecorino. When the water boils, add the pasta. It's done when it rises to the surface—probably 45 seconds to 1 minute.

Place the pasta in a serving dish, then melt a knob of butter into it. Top with thick lines of pecorino and oregano.

SNAPSHOTS OF EATING AND COOKING

Just after high school, I am visiting my half-Italian distant cousins in Rome. I am eating porcini pasta in a trattoria on a cobblestone road somewhere deep in Trastevere. There are two things I can see: pasta and mushrooms. But the layers of flavor just keep coming, and I gasp my way through the plate.

spring green lasagne

I loved lasagne as a kid. I'll admit it: I even thought Garfield comics were funny, and I loved the repeated lasagne jokes.

We made some pretty great lasagnes at the co-op house in college, with unusual but delicious layers like herbed goat cheese, caramelized onions, grilled squash, and so on. I'm sure someone made some bad ones with curry and tofu in them too.

Around the time I first started making my own pasta, I read some passage of Alice Waters's on lasagne: she says lasagne is at its most sublime made with fresh noodles, rolled out as thin as possible. I tried it, and (surprise, surprise) she's right.

Butter

1 tablespoon all-purpose flour

1½ cups whole milk

¼ cup whole milk yogurt

White pepper

1 large yellow onion

1 bunch parsley

1 bunch arugula

Juice from 1 lemon

Salt

Black pepper

Pine nuts or any other nuts you have handy (optional)

Parmesan

1 bunch spinach

½ bunch garlic scapes or green garlic

Olive oil

A variety of good cheeses (mozzarella, jack, a chalky goat cheese, aged pecorino)

8 to 10 lasagna noodles or homemade noodles cut in wide strips, such as the black pepper pasta (see page 152)

To make a light cream sauce, melt a pat of butter in a saucepan over medium heat, then whisk in the flour. Whisk until the flour starts to cook, just like you're making a béchamel. Add whole milk as the base, whisking until thickened, then add the whole milk yogurt, with the sauce bubbling away on low. Finally, add lots of white pepper. The result is a tangy, vaguely spicy white sauce.

Peel and dice the onion. Sweat it in a deep pan with butter, lifting the lid to stir frequently and making sure it really breaks down but doesn't brown.

For the green sauce, pull off the thicker bottom stems of the parsley. Wash and dry the tops. Repeat with the arugula (you're less likely to find tough stems here). Pile them into a food processor. Add the lemon juice, salt, black pepper, a handful of nuts, and some Parmesan. Blitz, then season to taste. Add 1 or 2 tablespoons of water to emulsify.

Prep the spinach: wash, trim the bottoms, and steam the leaves in a wok or large pan, until just starting to wilt. Let cool, then squeeze out the excess moisture and set aside.

For the garlic scapes, bring a wide saucepan of salted water to a boil (you'll also cook the pasta in it), and briefly blanch the garlic. After 1 minute in the boiling water, transfer to a hot cast-iron pan. Brush the exposed sides with olive oil, then turn them over with a spatula, pressing down to slightly char them. Remove from the heat, chop into pieces about 3 inches long, and set aside.

Grate, peel, or slice the cheeses—whatever is most appropriate for the ones you have.

In the boiling water, cook the pasta strips (cut to fit your baking dish), one at a time, for about 30 seconds each.

(Continued)

The Assembly Sequence:

Butter the baking dish,
  then arrange the first layer of pasta.
    Spread with white sauce.
      Add onions to the sauce layer.
        Sprinkle cheese over the onions.

Layer of pasta.
  Spread with white sauce.
    Add dollops of the green sauce.
      Arrange half of the garlic pieces.
      Sprinkle with cheese.

Layer of pasta.
  Spread with white sauce.
    Add the rest of the onions.
      Sprinkle with cheese.

Layer of pasta.
  Spread thickly with the green sauce.
    Arrange spinach over it.
      Sprinkle with cheese.

Layer of pasta.
  Spread with white sauce.
    Arrange remaining garlic pieces.
      Top with lots more cheese.

Cover with foil and bake at 400 degrees F for 20 minutes. Remove the foil and bake for another 20 to 25 minutes, or until the edges are crisping and the cheese is entirely melty and bubbling in places. Top with toasted nuts of some kind. (I would not, under normal circumstances, have invested in pine nuts, but I was gifted a 2-pound bag of them and thus got into the habit of using them liberally during times like these.)

bucatini with green garlic, butter, parmesan, and chili flakes

Weeknight suppers for me are often pasta, one featured vegetable, and some combination of dressings (but rarely a sauce). I like to use the ease and simplicity of this format to learn something about that featured vegetable and to start cooking knowing that the result will be satisfying. Sometimes it will be much more than satisfying: thrilling, even, as was the case with this green garlic bucatini. I've been making the classic spaghetti with garlic, chili, and Parmesan for years, sometimes with bread crumbs, anchovies, or clams. This recipe was an extension of that technique, after I discovered an unintentional garlic patch in my spring garden. The first time I made it was on a stormy night in May for a casual, improvised dinner with my roommate. We had it with some cheaper pinot noir and a purple asparagus salad (see page 64).

A few pieces green garlic

Butter

Bucatini pasta (hollow spaghetti)

Salt

Olive oil

Parmesan

Red pepper flakes

Slice the green garlic into discs, like you might with leeks, stopping right before the greenest tops. Melt enough butter to entirely coat your frying pan, plus some extra. Pop the green garlic into the pan, holding each piece in your fingers and squeezing so the layers pop out as they go into the pan. Stir to coat, then cook over medium-low until they are bright green and have made the butter quite garlicky.

Boil some generously salted water, add your pasta and check after 8 minutes. It's finished when a noodle is exactly how you want it.

While the pasta is cooking and the green garlic is sautéing, cut the green garlic tops lengthwise into very thin strips with your sharpest, thinnest knife. Get out a baking sheet. Pour a little olive oil into your hand, then pick up the bunch of garlic strips, rolling them back and forth in your hand to lightly distribute the oil. Lay the strips on the baking sheet and broil for about 90 seconds, taking them out when they are all crisping up and some pieces have just started to blacken.

(Continued)

Drain the pasta and toss it with the cooked green garlic and butter. Add a pinch of good red pepper flakes. Grate Parmesan generously over the top. Toss half of the green garlic strips in with the pasta, and save the other half.

Distribute into bowls and top with the remaining green garlic strips. Stir some into the curl of pasta, so they curl as well, mirroring the circles in the bowl; leave others to stay crispy on top. Finish with extra Parmesan.

fresh tomato sauce, basic spaghetti

I first came up with this sauce for a late-August Secret Restaurant dinner during our first year. I was, at the time, pulling the concept out of thin air, and it was so ridiculously delicious that I've been methodically refining it every summer since.

Onions, a small amount	Balsamic vinegar
Plenty of garlic	Cooked spaghetti or other favorite pasta
Plenty olive oil	Parmesan
Salt	Fresh oregano, basil, or thyme
Quite a few tomatoes	

Cut onions into pieces a ¼ inch thick, then chop them finely. Slice the garlic thinly, leave it out in the air for a few minutes, then mince it.

Coat a heavy-bottomed stockpot with olive oil, add the onion and a dash of salt and cook over medium-high heat until translucent. Add the garlic and stir together, lowering the heat to medium low.

Continue cooking on medium-low, without browning either the garlic or the onions, trying to encourage everything to break down progressively. Cover the pan briefly to help sweat the moisture out of the onions, then remove the lid and stir to let the steam out.

De-stem and chop all the tomatoes. Toss them into the pot with the onions and increase the heat to high. Stirring constantly, watch for the moment the tomatoes bubble into a boil, then immediately switch off the heat.

Drain the contents of the stockpot over a mesh sieve placed on top of a sturdy bowl. Press the mixture repeatedly to squeeze out as much juice as you can (a grill spatula is perfect for this). Let it drip. Scrape the bottom of the sieve. Press, scrape, press, scrape, and so on.

When it has drained satisfactorily, reserve the barely cooked tomatoes, onions, and garlic in a separate bowl, and return the tomato juice to the pan.

Cook the juice over high heat, stirring constantly. Reduce, scraping the sides if and when it starts to stick. Eventually it will start to thicken. Begin to taste

(Continued)

around this time, when it is sweetening and intensifying. Keep going on high heat.

When the juice is bubbling so much that you can see the sugars in it start to become syrup, add some glugs of balsamic vinegar and turn off the heat. Stir and let sit for a minute to cool. Taste it—if it's sublime, it's done. If it isn't, turn the heat back up and keep cooking down until the flavor has reached the perfect concentration.

Mix with the reserved tomatoes, onions, and garlic. It should be intensely sweet yet tangy, filled with umami. Salt further to taste.

Serve the sauce over the spaghetti, with just a little fresh Parmesan and chopped fresh oregano, torn basil, or a sprinkling of thyme.

penne with eggplant, spinach, walnuts, parmesan, and bread crumbs

When I made this dish for the first time, I had pulled in several last harvests from the fall garden. The day had threatened ice pellets. With school canceled, I had spent the morning making cloche covers as the wind howled, then running back inside to cook the last batch of candied tomatoes, and so on. I took a break for lunch to make this eggplant pasta. That summer was long and hot, so the eggplants had been producing actively since early July. It was then mid-November. I cooked the pasta, thinking about all the solitary eggplant pasta I'd eaten that year. These eggplants in my kitchen would probably be the last for a long time.

The ice pellets and crystallized snow were falling by that time. A Nigel Slater–inspired moment presented itself. I descended the back staircase to visit the bed of spinaches, sown with old seed and not in time at that. I hadn't had enough materials to make a cover for this garden bed, and so sacrificed it to the weather. The plants were lying sideways, dying in the snow drifts. I pulled them all out and carried them upstairs, ice melting into my bare hands as I went. I washed and trimmed them, saving the most intact leaves, sometimes leaving the plant whole if the root was tender enough.

---

1 or more eggplants, depending on how many you're serving	Small handful of walnuts
Salt	1 bunch baby spinach
Penne pasta	Black pepper
Olive oil	Handful of bread crumbs
	Handful of coarsely grated Parmesan

Cut the eggplant into cubes, sprinkle with salt, and let it hang out in a colander for a bit.

Boil water with a generous quantity of salt. Cook the penne for at least 10 minutes. It always seems to take a bit longer than other dried pastas.

Heat a glug of olive oil in a cast-iron pan until it shimmers. Then add the eggplant, tossing to coat. Fry on each side until it goes golden, then reduce the heat to medium-low and continue to "melt" until a sort of eggplant ragu is

(Continued)

created naturally in the pan. When it is done, crumble in the walnuts and fold them into the eggplant. Turn the heat down to low.

Wash the baby spinach.

When the pasta is done, drain it, and return to the saucepan where it was cooked. Immediately scrape the entire contents (extra oil and all) of the eggplant-walnut pan into it. Add the baby spinach, and toss so it gets wilted by the steam. Crack in some good black pepper. Put a lid on the pan and let it hang out for 1 minute.

If you happen to have walnut country bread around, the walnut bread crumbs really make the whole thing sing. Regardless, have prepared some of your ideal bread crumbs and a whole mess of coarsely grated (this is one of the few times in the book that I feel strongly about the consistency) Parmesan. Uncover the pan and throw in the bread crumbs and half the Parmesan. Stir, and tip out into serving dishes or a serving bowl. Top with a few more crumbled walnuts and the rest of the Parmesan.

SNAPSHOTS OF EATING AND COOKING

Making risotto some winter night in my home kitchen in Portland: I lid the pot once it is done and move on to the salad. Sofie keeps sneaking back to the pot and eating more of the risotto. She won't stop. She's laughing and grinning and putting her spoon back into the pot and saying over and over again, "I hate it, it's terrible."

beery mac and cheese

As a preschool teacher, I end up talking about mac and cheese nearly every day. As a child myself, mac and cheese was easily my favorite meal. This is a grown-up version, easily adaptable to your own preferences.

Conchiglie pasta (big-shelled macaroni)

1 shallot

Butter

Beer (something distinctly beery-tasting, like a bock beer, amber ale, or malty brown; you want the taste to impart itself, so don't shy away from heavily hopped or malted beers)

White cheddar from Vermont, Oregon, or the U.K.

Gouda or other fine melting cheese

1 tablespoon all-purpose flour

1½ cups whole milk

Mustard

Salt

Cook the pasta in heavily salted boiling water for about 10 minutes. Drain, return to the pot with a splash of the cooking water and place the lid over it.

Mince the shallot. Heat your smallest cast-iron skillet. Melt butter in the skillet, enough to really coat the bottom. Add the minced shallot and cook on medium-high for a minute or two. The edges may start to brown. Turn the heat down to medium, stir a bit, and watch it start to go translucent. When the shallot pieces are soft and "done," turn the heat up to high again. Just as the moisture is reducing significantly and the edges are starting to brown again, pour in a healthy splash of beer, agitate the pan, and turn the heat off.

Grate the cheddar. Set some aside for the top. Grate some Gouda now if you have that too.

In a heavy-bottomed saucepan, melt ¼ to ½ stick butter. When the butter starts to foam, add the flour. Whisk immediately to incorporate and continue whisking to make a roux. When the mixture is smooth and starting to go slightly golden, add the milk in a slow stream, whisking all the while. Stop and whisk some more, keeping the heat under the pan around medium. As the milk temperature catches up to the butter and the flour, it should bubble a bit and start to thicken. Keep whisking. When it has really started to thicken, pour in another generous amount of beer. It will froth up, just keep whisking. When it settles down and is still smooth—turn the heat down to low. Keep stirring for a minute or two, and then once the mixture has cooled a little (this is essential), add half of the shredded cheddar. Let this cheese melt into the mixture. Add the shallot mixture from the small pan. Whisk to incorporate.

Add a good teaspoon (or more to taste) of your favorite mustard, and the second half of the cheese. Whisk slowly until the sauce reaches the perfect consistency (not lumpy, not too thick).

In a baking pan, layer half of the cooked pasta, drizzle with half the sauce, then add the second half of the pasta, and pour in the remaining sauce. Top with the Gouda and reserved cheddar. Bake at 425 degrees F for 15 to 30 minutes, or until the top is crisp and the inside is bubbling.

ACCOMPANIMENTS

turnips with wakame and maitake

On the farm in New Hampshire, the one that never became our communal dream home (but was, for one summer), we had too many turnips. I was including turnips in nearly every meal. One night, with no guests around to impress, and a sudden rainstorm, I made a whole meal with turnips. We ate bowls of sour cream and onion turnip mash with deeply roasted turnips on top, then a pile of garlic buttery wilted chard, and sunflower seed gravy. The power was out, the barn was dark, and we only had a couple of candles. Someone knocked one over as they passed the bottle of cheap wine around through the shadows.

That night really cemented my love for turnips. This side dish was made on the heels of the big post-holidays turnip phase, to go with cleansing brothy soups and plates of noodles and greens.

A few small or 1 large maitake mushroom	Oyster sauce
Oil	Purple winter turnips
Kombu ponzu or regular ponzu	Dried wakame

Place your maitakes (if it's one large maitake, break it up into smaller pieces) in a bowl, and dress with oil, ponzu (there is a fancier ponzu made with kombu that is particularly delicious), and oyster sauce. Then transfer the dressed maitakes to a roasting tin but reserve the bowl. You'll use it again. Place under a low broiler for about 4 minutes or in the oven at 300 degrees F for 20 minutes, or until the edges are slightly crispy. Tear the crisp-edged maitakes up into smaller pieces and set aside.

Cut the turnips into large bite-size pieces, then boil for 5 minutes in salted water. Remove and rinse under cold water, pulling the skin off with your fingers.

Dress the turnips with oil in the reserved bowl, tossing to evenly coat, then cook in a frying pan over medium-low heat for a few minutes on each side.

Place the turnips, unseasoned, in a serving dish. Dribble some ponzu and oyster sauce over them. Reheat the maitakes by briefly rolling them around in the hot frying pan the turnips just came from. Toss them evenly, then add the dried wakame. Some of it will loosen with the moisture, some pieces will stay crispy—a delightful combination.

smothered savoy cabbage

I started making cabbage this way by watching Sofie and her friend
Bryan making it over and over again, then trying with a delicate
savoy cabbage. Later I found out that they got started doing Marcella
Hazan's version, featured in *Genius Recipes*. It is so good it has a place
at any table, at any meal.

Butter	1 smaller savoy cabbage
Olive oil	Splash of alcohol
1 yellow onion	Good vinegar
Good salt	

Melt a large pat of butter into a glug of olive oil in a large sauté pan, over
medium heat.

Peel and thinly slice the onion, adding it, with a pinch of good salt, to the
pan. Stir to coat the onion in the fat and cook over medium-high heat without
touching it until it starts to brown on the bottom.

Meanwhile, clean and prep the savoy cabbage, chopping it into nice strips.

When the onion has begun to brown, scrape it away from the center of the
pan, leaving a circle in the middle. Pour in some alcohol—beer (a pilsner or
saison would be best), white wine, or white vermouth. Stir to deglaze the
onions, then lower the heat to medium low.

Add the cabbage, stirring to mix evenly, then cover. After 3 to 5 minutes, stir
the cabbage and onions again. Replace the cover, but this time leave a space
to let steam out. After another few minutes, add good vinegar (the variety
doesn't matter so much as the quality—muscatel is my favorite, tarragon white
wine vinegar, and so on). Stir once more, and turn the heat down to low.

Continue to cook for nearly 1 hour, stirring every 10 to 15 minutes to make
sure it doesn't start to burn. The result will be a purplish-brown, unctuous
mixture that is wonderful on bread with nothing else, stirred into rice, as part
of a Euro-zone mezze platter, or as a side dish for meats and fishes.

winter pickles

This is a basic guideline for good homemade quick pickles. It can be used with vegetables and fruits from the other seasons as well.

---

3 Bosc pears	3 scarlet turnips
3 leeks	Distilled white vinegar
1 small or ½ large head cauliflower	Apple cider vinegar
1½ to 2 fennel bulbs	White wine vinegar
1 bunch rainbow carrots	Mustard seeds
1 head celery	Coriander seeds
3 black radishes	

Prepare the pears and vegetables in a way that suits your tastes for shape and texture. For example, I took out the cores of the pears but tried to keep the long shape, including the stems on some pieces. I peeled the carrots but not the black radishes. It's also a good move to pare off the grittier skin on the outsides of the scarlet turnips. Stuff quart mason jars with the produce.

Fill a tall stockpot and one-quarter of the way up with distilled white vinegar. Fill it another quarter of the way up with water so it is half full. Add generous splashes of the other vinegars, stir, and bring to a boil.

Add the seeds. When they've been rolling in the boiling liquid long enough to start to burst (just some of them), ladle the liquid out into a funnel perched over the mason jars.

Cover with clean lids, fasten with clean rings, pop in the fridge, and let the produce pickle for at least a couple of days. These keep, crispness intact, for a good month or two.

This winter selection is delicious served with homemade crackers, good mustard, and honey.

SNAPSHOTS OF EATING AND COOKING

Traveling in Europe with Asher, ragtag style. In the English countryside, we eat traditional kedgeree (smoked fish and rice) on an usually warm November afternoon. A month later, in Poland, we're taken to a Christmas market in a medieval square where we eat smoked mountain cheeses, heated over a fire and topped with cranberry sauce, then chased with hot spiced wine. The snow falls, first on our noses, making them colder, and then in our cups, evaporating instantly and knocking our senses wide open.

roasted bitter greens with bread crumbs and porcini

We were in Seattle having dinner with Sofie's dad. There was a special salad kind of like this, but simpler: radicchio, bread crumbs, anchovies, Parmesan. It was perfect and really hit the spot. As I was eating it, I thought about how good it would be with porcini mushrooms. I also wanted it to still be smoking hot—to eat it from the pan. So a day or two later I made it my way, with the porcini and even more bread crumbs, and I ate it from the pan.

---

1 bunch bitter greens, such as radicchio, dandelion, or mustard	½ salt-packed anchovy, or 1 whole oil-packed anchovy
Leftover good bread	Red pepper flakes
Olive oil	A few porcini mushrooms
Good salt	Parmesan

Preheat the oven to 425 degrees F. Wash and dry the greens. Put them in a deep cast-iron pan or baking dish.

Break up the bread in a food processor, leaving the pieces slightly larger than normal bread crumbs. Drizzle with olive oil, sprinkle with good salt, toss, and place on a baking sheet in the oven while it's heating up.

If using a salt-packed anchovy, wash and remove the bones. Chop the anchovy and mix it with 1 teaspoon olive oil and some red pepper flakes.

Brush and trim the porcinis into bite-size pieces. Fry on medium heat in a shallow pan with olive oil and a sprinkling of good salt, until they are colored appetizingly. While cooking the mushrooms, grate a bunch of Parmesan.

Take out the toasted bread crumbs and put the greens in the oven. Bake for 5 to 10 minutes, checking to see when they're starting to dry and "cook" but still have striking color. At this stage, toss them with the anchovy and oil and put back in the oven for another 3 to 5 minutes.

Toss the bread crumbs, roasted greens, and Parmesan together. Top with pieces of smoking hot porcini. Eat immediately, preferably from the pan.

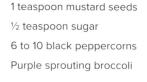

pickled purple sprouting broccoli

A lovely pickle. Another purple vegetable staying purple. These are excellent tucked into sandwiches, tossed into salads, and snacked on with soft cheeses.

1 part white vinegar	1 teaspoon mustard seeds
1 part rice vinegar	½ teaspoon sugar
½ part apple cider vinegar	6 to 10 black peppercorns
1 teaspoon salt	Purple sprouting broccoli

In a medium-small saucepan, heat the vinegars, salt, mustard seeds, sugar, and peppercorns over medium heat.

Separate the florets from the stalks of the purple sprouting broccoli, then stuff them into a clean quart mason jar.

When the mixture has slowly risen to a boil, turn off the heat and let it cool for about a minute, then pour it slowly into the jar over the broccoli. Seal, store in the fridge, and eat the next day or any time within 3 weeks.

Yes, they will stay purple and taste delicious!

dark rye, oozing cheese, pickled purple sprouting broccoli

Get some of that extremely dense Bavarian rye bread from an international market or your discerning local grocer.

Select the best soft cheese around (in this case, I had been gifted some Harbison, a beautiful cheese from Jasper Hill, in Vermont).

Spread the cheese, skipping the rind, onto the slices of rye bread. Top with one or two pieces of Pickled Purple Sprouting Broccoli (opposite page).

cheese board with fiddleheads and morels

A word about cheese boards:

They can be mind-blowing or mildly disappointing in restaurants. They will always be expensive. Yet a good one at home can actually be hard to make. Most often cheesemongers at grocery stores try to upsell you on more of a thirty-two-dollars-per-pound cheese than you need, either by only presenting it in pre-cut portions or by cutting large slices without asking! The best practice is to find a smaller cheese counter you know and trust. Maybe they don't have every option in the world, but they have the best options. Tell them you are making a single cheese plate and that you'd like five quite small portions of cheese. Tell them what you are cooking to go with or after it, and whether you want diversity (sheep, goat, cow, soft, hard, runny) or a tasting of similar perfect compliments (five Italian pecorinos of varying ages and textures or something). Ask for tastes of what they suggest. If you don't love it, don't feel pressured into getting it just because the professional made the suggestion.

After doing this a few times and creating some successful cheese plates, you'll get to know some favorite kinds of fancy cheese and keywords that will lead you to more successful purchases in the future.

The best cheeses in my book:

Anything picked by Neal's Yard in London. Several Neal's Yard cheeses are exported to discerning cheesemongers.

Jasper Hill in Greensboro, Vermont. They age others' cheeses and make their own. All are exceptional. Harbison, pictured on page 175, is one of the best in the world.

Cascade Creamery in Trout Lake, Washington. They make aged raw milk cheeses in the English tradition.

Point Reyes Farmstead Cheese Company in Point Reyes, CA. French style.

Franklin's Teleme in San Luis Obispo, CA. A one-of-a-kind, gorgeous, perfect, melting cheese. I've also discovered many delightful cheeses by asking for Franklin's when they are all out, and trying good substitutions.

(Continued)

Fiddlehead ferns

Morel mushrooms

Butter

Olive oil

Good salt

Garlic

Favorite bread

Leonora (Leon, Spain) a crumbly goat's cheese with a creamy layer and rind

Pecornio Di Penza (Italy) a fresh, soft sheep's cheese

Taleggio (Italy) a classic soft cow's cheese

Crucolo (Italy) a medium-hard cow's cheese

Franklin's Teleme (San Luis Obispo, California) a soft cow's cheese

Coastal cheddar (Ford Farms, England) a crumbly and medium-hard cow's cheese

---

Get a medium shallow pan going with boiling water. Wash your fiddleheads by putting them in a metal bowl, covering them with water and shaking the pieces around to get the dirt to float to the surface. Pour off the water and little bits of forest and repeat a few times as needed. Salt the boiling water generously and add the fiddleheads. Cook for 90 seconds, then remove to an ice bath.

Preheat the oven to 400 degrees F. Brush the morels as best you can. You should check the insides for bugs, and the best method I've found is to tear a bit of a paper napkin, wet it, wrap it around a finger, then sweep out the insides of the mushrooms with that finger. Melt a large pat of butter and combine with a tablespoon or two of olive oil, depending on how many morels you are preparing. Pour the fat over the mushrooms in a small roasting tin. Toss to coat, then add a tablespoon or two of water to the bottom of the pan for steaming. Cover with aluminum foil and place in the oven.

Meanwhile, remove the fiddleheads from the ice bath and gently sauté with garlic and butter.

Bake the mushrooms for 15 to 20 minutes, until they have cooked down and the fat has been totally absorbed. Remove the foil, add some good salt, then place under the broiler for 60 to 90 seconds—just until the tops get a slight bit crispy.

Combine the fiddleheads and morels so they absorb one another's excess buttery juices. Serve with the cheeses and a favorite bread.

One spring Sofie and I were in Vermont for a week, and it seemed like every other day we ate fiddleheads, ramps, morels—or all three, as they were abundant and affordable. We were driving around with Jasper Hill cheeses in the car, obtained nearest to the source. On the way from town to town, we'd pick up a perfect rustic bread, and at our destination would eat a dreamy spread like this.

summer sun carpaccio

One summer, I hosted biweekly garden party potlucks. I would make one large dish, using whatever was overly abundant in the garden, and encourage friends to bring complementary dishes. One week it was yellow crookneck squash and golden beets. I improvised this recipe the day before the potluck and have made it faithfully every summer since. This past year, I made it for a group of friends in Maine to accompany a ribollita soup on a hot, rainy night.

5 small golden beets	Olive oil
2 yellow summer squash	Good salt
1 large lemon	White wine vinegar

Bring a pot of water to a boil. Clean and scrub the beets under running water. Trim the rough ends and add them to the pot. Boil for 30 to 45 minutes, or until a fork goes in easily. Drain, then (when cool enough to handle) run under cold water, rubbing until the skins come off.

Thinly slice the yellow summer squash with your best, thinnest knife or a mandolin. Salt generously, toss, and leave in a colander for about 10 minutes. The water will be drawn out of the squash.

When the beets have cooled a bit, slice them even thinner than the squash with your best, thinnest knife or a mandolin. Zest and juice the lemon.

In a glass bowl, mix the squash and beets and add the lemon juice. Add 1 tablespoon olive oil and two pinches of good salt.

Lay the dressed pieces in a nice dish and scatter the lemon zest over them. Cover and refrigerate, letting the lemon work its magic for a few hours, or 1 to 2 days.

Uncover, let it return to room temperature, and drizzle with some white wine vinegar and just a touch more olive oil. Taste. Perhaps a little flaky salt?

romanesco with leeks and sage

Romanesco is a delightful vegetable, but it doesn't belong in many of the places where cauliflower and broccoli do. It is better standing mostly on its own, like in this dish where it is quietly supported by melted leeks and crisp sage.

1 head Romanesco broccoli	Handful of sage leaves
1 leek	Oil
Butter	White wine vinegar
Salt	

Wash the Romanesco under cold running water, then separate into florets. Wash and slice the leek, reserving the green top.

Cook the Romanesco florets in boiling salted water for 3 to 5 minutes, until bright green and just tender. Remove, chop half of them and set aside.

Melt a large pat of butter, add the leek, and sprinkle with salt. Cook the leek until soft and translucent, then add the Romanesco.

Cover, turn the heat down to low, and let the Romanesco steam through and get infused with leek butter. The leeks will start to caramelize; if you don't like this, don't cover the pan and just keep stirring.

Heat a separate wide nonstick pan. Stack and slice the sage leaves. Add them to the dry pan and cook until they start to crisp and curl, then remove swiftly before they burn.

Thinly slice the leek top. Add to the dry pan and cook, as you did the sage leaves. Add a bit of oil if they start to blacken before cooking all the way through. Remove and set aside.

At the last minute, add some splashes of the vinegar to Romanesco-leek mixture, and then toss with the sage and leek tops.

argyle grilled eggplant

My college housemate Ethan, whose Secret Restaurant project in New York inspired my own, taught me how to do eggplant this way. It works as a side dish, a sandwich filling, a pizza topping, the basis for classic eggplant Parmesan, part of a curry or a stew—really, there is infinite variability. It is a true celebration of this underdog vegetable.

Large globe eggplant	Olive oil
Salt	Balsamic vinegar

Slice the eggplant into ½- to ¼-inch medallions. Move them to a colander, sprinkle with salt, and leave them for about 20 minutes while the salt draws the moisture out. Move them to a casserole dish or roasting tin, pat dry with a clean towel, and dress with lots of olive oil. When some has been absorbed, splash the dish with balsamic vinegar. Leave alone for another 10 to 20 minutes.

Heat a cast-iron grill pan over medium-high heat until a flick of water will instantly evaporate.

You need a good pair of tongs for this job. Pick up the pieces of eggplant and lay them gently on the hot grill. Leave them completely alone for about 2 minutes, then pick them up delicately to make sure they haven't stuck. If any have stuck, use a regular flat metal spatula to scrape the underside and lift the piece up. Cook the other side for about half the time of the first side, keeping a watchful eye (and watchful tonged hand) on them the whole time. To encourage them to

cook down, you can gently press the top with the spatula, and you'll see the water hiss out and evaporate on all sides.

Place the finished pieces in a dish in a warm oven, like you might do for pancakes, until you've got a great hot pile of them to use however you like.

spiced onions

A cheap taqueria near my house won me over when I discovered the roasted onions in the salsa bar. This is my home re-creation. These are amazing stuffed into burritos, as part of a taco toppings spread, worked into stir-fry dishes, tossed into a salad, or even stirred into mac and cheese.

Small to medium onions	Chili powder
Oil	Cumin
Salt	Paprika
Sugar	Old Bay

Grease the bottom of a roasting tin, then fill it with the whole onions. Bake at 425 degrees F for 30 to 45 minutes, or until the onions are puffed up and clearly going tender. Take the roasting tin out of the oven, and let the onions cool for 15 minutes or so.

Get a pair of culinary scissors and pick up each onion, stabbing it with the scissors and cutting until you can easily pull off the skin. Drop the mostly whole onions back in the tin, and repeat until all the onions are skinless.

Then, using the scissors, slice them into progressively smaller pieces, filling the tin with bite-size pieces of onion. Dress with oil, salt, and a little sugar. Then season the top layer heavily with all the spices. Return the roasting tin to the oven and bake for another 20 minutes.

Remove the tin, scraping the bottom where some onions are sure to be caramelizing and sticking. After stirring them around, season the top layer again, heavily, and return the roasting tin to the oven. Bake for another 30 minutes, taking the tin out and agitating the onions every 10 minutes or so to ensure even cooking.

Keep going until you have perfect (to you) onions.

super fresh salsa

Towards the end of summer, the year of the garden party potlucks, there was a week where I could see nearly everything in one half of the garden going into a fresh salsa.

One of the conversation topics had been. "It's so nice to go to potlucks where it's not just a table full of chips." This time, I sent out a message saying, "Hey! This time I want you all to bring chips!"

The chard stems are the sneaky, unusual, and exciting element. Their color, texture, and flavor is extremely well suited to salsa.

Several varieties of tomatoes at the height of summer	Chard
	1 spicy pepper
Salt	Red wine vinegar
Onions	Flat-leaf parsley, cilantro, or salad burnet
Garlic	

De-stem and slice all the tomatoes on your largest cutting board. Place near the sink. Leave for a few minutes so the watery excess juices and seeds can settle onto the board. Lift the tomatoes into a bowl. Tip the juice and seeds into the sink, wash the cutting board, put the tomatoes back, and chop them pretty finely. Remove to the bowl again and salt generously.

Chop the onions and garlic. Strip the leaves from the chard, saving for another use, and dice the stems. Slice the pepper in half, scoop out and discard the seeds, and dice. Add everything to the bowl with the tomatoes and combine. Drizzle in the red wine vinegar. Let sit for at least 30 minutes.

Chop the herbs, fold them in to the salsa, and adjust the seasonings to taste. Add a drop of prepared hot sauce or a dash of cayenne if it is not spicy enough, a touch of sugar if it is too acidic, some more salt if it is not savory enough; at this point, adjust it entirely to your tastes.

candied tomatoes

My first taste of a tomato candied this way was in mid-spring, long before the beginning of tomato season. The tomatoes had come into Sofie's possession through a distributor of unsold grocery store produce—loads of tomatoes from Mexico, otherwise left to rot. She was wooing me then, with good food left and right in little glass Pyrex containers packed with vibrant flavors. Right before I tasted them she said, "Just be prepared. Nothing else I make will ever be as good." I can still remember that first taste and how it felt like the flavor wasn't ever going to end.

Apparently the technique originates from Italian grandmothers using the residual heat in wood-burning ovens, after making breads or roasting meats. As the heat in the oven gradually decreases, the tomatoes cook further and further into an unctuous perfection.

Cherry tomatoes are absolutely the best for this, but really any tomatoes you want to process and preserve are fine

Olive oil

Salt

Sugar

Balsamic vinegar or red wine vinegar

De-stem the tomatoes completely. For anything other than the smallest cherry tomato, cut them in halves or quarters. Plum tomatoes or larger tomatoes need to be cut into several smaller pieces, and some of the excess juice and seeds sacrificed.

When all the tomatoes are prepped in a mixing bowl, drizzle quite generously with olive oil and stir. Sprinkle with salt and the tiniest amount of sugar, add a dribble or two of balsamic vinegar and/or red wine, then stir again.

Pour into a roasting tin or a glass or ceramic casserole dish. I've had good results with all, but the cooking times vary: the thicker the vessel, the longer the process. A good metal roasting tin with a serious patina from lots of scraped pan juices is the best, I think.

Roast first at 400 degrees F for 30 minutes. Second, at 350 degrees F for another 30 minutes. Third, at 300 degrees F for a final 30 to 45 minutes. After that first 30 minutes, you want to check them every 20 minutes or so and stir, as the juices will start to caramelize around the edges and you want

to scrape those pieces back into the oily sauce that forms around the whole tomatoes and has the wildly unctuous flavor.

When the tomatoes are done, let them cool completely, then pile them into a jar. Scrape out every last drop of umami-rich oil-sauce with a rubber spatula to cover the whole tomatoes. If this doesn't really cover the tomatoes in the jar, pour more olive oil on top. Eat from the fridge for 3 weeks, or freeze indefinitely. I like to make several small jars throughout tomato season, then ration them out over the rest of the year.

On the day you make them, save some of the tomato oil and sticky pieces of candied tomato in the pans. Just for fun, cook a single portion of rigatoni in boiling, well-salted water for about 12 minutes, until perfectly al dente. Drain, and then toss the pasta in the pans. Get in there with your spatula and get the last of this flavor blast onto the pasta. Season with just a little salt and eat it right then and there.

bread and fancy butter (or something like it)

On a morning with a bit of spare time, go walking to find an ideal loaf of bread.

Choose the bread based on the fancy butter or other topping you have planned. Choose the bread with your appetite. Should it be chewy and soft—a middle ground for your palate? Should it be sour and complex, more of a mouthful? Would seeds or olives or herbs in the bread enhance or distract from what you'll be eating it with? The idea is to eat the freshest bread, at the height of your desire for it.

On the way home, smell the bread. Take one, but just one, tear off the side to tease yourself for the whole experience. Maybe you're going to eat it right away with unsalted butter, flaky salt, and preserves. Or with a creamy cheese and rose jam. Or with some fancy butter, like anchovy-pimento butter, whipped up fresh from some wildly delicious European stuff.

Maybe it will be part of lunch, the lone accompaniment to a bowl of soup. Maybe it is to be a pick-me-up after a session in the garden, a reward to look forward to, with a dish of olive oil, garlic, salt, and pepper for dunking.

When the time comes to eat the bread, create your perfect setting, keeping things simple. Be outside if you can, taking in the light and the trees or the brick wall or the neighbor's porch or whatever is in your view.

Eat the bread, slowly, and let yourself have more than most people think is okay.

BREAKFASTS

porridge with ginger and currants

This makes enough for one person to have a large, filling bowl or two people to have small, sturdy bowls to accompany other breakfast items. After making porridge so frequently in the fall and winter, one year I decided to just really go for it, and I got the traditional Scottish porridge stirring tool—the spurtle. Laugh at me why don't you! But now that I have one, I'll never go back. They are available for less than ten dollars, primarily online and all the way from the UK.

Small handful of crystallized ginger

Small handful of dried currants

Large handful or shallow bowlful of oats

Good fine salt

Your favorite oatmeal spoon

A nice bowl

Sweetener

Slice your ginger cubes into 4 or 5 thinner pieces each. Portion out your currants. Have them both at the ready.

Fill a heavy-bottomed saucepan or copper-bottomed Revere Ware with enough water to be about 1 inch deep, and place it on the stove over high heat. A gas stove offers astoundingly more control in porridge-making than an electric one. When you sense the water is getting hot, add the oats and stir clockwise with a spurtle. The handle-side of a wooden spoon will do just fine too.

If making plain porridge, you'd commence stirring non-stop now, but when adding dried fruit that you want to plump up (the currants) or a flavor you want to affect every bite (the ginger), take this different approach:

Add your ginger and currants, and then just let the oats start to cook for a minute here. There is still enough water in the pan that they won't start to stick. When you see large bubbles around the sides and small bubbles in the center, add your healthy pinch of fine salt and begin stirring in earnest.

As you notice the water starting to decrease in volume and the oats starting to cream a bit, reduce the heat to medium, and continue stirring and scraping the pan.

It should take anywhere from 3 to 5 minutes from here.

You want the porridge to get a thick, creamy consistency that will hold its shape in a spoon rather than rolling off back into the bowl.

Tip into your favorite bowl (wooden or a tall ceramic, warmed with hot water perhaps) and taste. Depending on how your ratio of oats to ginger and currants works out, you may find you want a touch more sweetness. Ginger syrup or even a pinch of golden unrefined sugar will do.

This porridge needn't be topped by butter, milk, brown sugar, jam, or any of the other traditional toppings (though they are all delicious). The ginger provides a continuous, warming heat, even after the porridge has cooled down, and the currants a tangy sweetness.

Eat the porridge in your favorite chair with a cup of coffee in your favorite mug. Consider setting aside a solid 20 minutes to consume these things in the morning, with a plan to read a chapter of your book or gaze out the window with early daydreams.

muesli

I remember eating muesli sometimes as a child, but my renewed taste for it comes from making the best of things in horrible European hostels in 2012. The muesli itself wasn't exactly top-notch, but the eating of it was so pleasant and so much better than all the other options. Having a tall jar of this homemade stuff waiting for you every morning makes the week just fly by!

Note: Go with about one cup of "cereal" (the oats and flaked grains, mixed) per person.

⅔ cup oats

⅓ cup mixed flaked grain (Bob's Red Mill 10 grain porridge works really well—it contains spelt, rye, and all sorts of other good grains. These other grains are less digestible near-raw than oats, however. That's why I recommend less of them. You can also make your own mix from bulk bins at the co-op.)

Sunflower seeds

Golden raisins

Dried currants or other small, dark fruit: blueberries or black cherries, for instance

Best-quality milk (works with alternative milks too, but the thicker the better)

Turkish apricots

Dried pears

Dark brown sugar

Flaked or chopped almonds (the kind that are machine-cut so thin feel very elegant here, but any will do)

When you get up in the morning, before coffee or a shower or anything else, mix the oats, flaked grains, sunflower seeds, raisins, and currants in your favorite breakfast bowl.

Pour milk over it all, to about ½ inch higher than the cereal itself. Stir, pat down with your spoon, and leave the kitchen to do those other morning things: shower, dress, check your email, take the dog out, water the garden, start the coffee.

When about 30 minutes has passed (more is perfectly fine) chop the apricots and pears and toss them with the now mostly soaked cereal. Add a little more milk if you like. Top with a single spoonful of dark brown sugar and the almonds, stirring them in as you eat.

Take your bowl to a favorite spot, outside if the weather permits, and eat at your own pace with your own thoughts.

plums for breakfast

In the neighborhood of the first preschool where I worked, it felt like Italian plum trees lined every block. When the fruit was ripe, I would escape the building on my ten-minute breaks to scurry down the surrounding streets, filling my canvas tote bag with plums. At home I would roast the plums to eat hot over ice cream or put into a spice cake. The leftovers I would save for breakfast.

Small frosty blue Italian plums	Knob of ginger
Sugar	Yogurt
Lemon	Granola

Gather the small, frosty blue Italian plums in September from some tree that is just dripping with fruit. Wash them and cut the stones out, then toss the pieces into a roasting tin. Sprinkle with a handful or two of sugar. Juice a whole lemon and toss it over the sugary plums. Peel and thinly slice the ginger, then disperse it throughout the tin. Bake at 375 degrees F for 30 to 45 minutes, stirring the pan every 10 minutes or so to ensure even cooking. Scrape the plums into a jar and let cool completely. Eat them for breakfast the next couple of mornings topped with yogurt and granola.

harvest time granola

I lived at the college co-op house a full three years, the absolute maximum possible (you had to live on campus at least a year). During that time, the "house granola"—making job switched hands many times. It never became my job, but I tried to take the best of what I watched and tasted and use those ideas and techniques later.

I'm also from Eugene, Oregon, a place where granola is actually considered a staple food. The way people in the heartland have beef and people in California have avocados and citrus, we have granola.

Rolled oats	Honey
Hazelnuts	Maple syrup
Almonds	Golden raisins
Cashews	Chopped dried apricots
Pumpkin seeds	Best fresh apples or pears
Sesame seeds	Yogurt, kefir, or milk
Oil	

Mix the rolled oats, nuts, and seeds evenly in a large mixing bowl. Don't put in the dried fruit yet! A frequent homemade granola blooper is burning the raisins and apricots.

Mix the oil, honey, and maple syrup in a smaller bowl, whisking together with a fork. Drizzle over the oats, nuts, and seeds, stirring to incorporate. Drizzle on some more honey, to form clusters and add an every-other-bite sweetness.

Pour the mixture into parchment-lined roasting tins and bake at 300 degrees F for 40 to 60 minutes. Take the pans out and stir midway through. Let cool completely, then combine with the golden raisins and apricots and pour into tall sealable jars.

Eat the granola with slices of fresh autumn apples or pears and the best live-culture yogurt, creamy jersey milk, kefir, or high-quality nut milk.

lumberjack slam

The college co-op house was called The Townhouse. It wasn't like a townhouse in a city at all though—the name just meant "a house, in the town." It was a really tall Victorian house, on a hill, looking down on a historic train station. Weekend breakfast was the one time when almost everyone was around and everyone needed to eat, but no official communal meal was planned. Everyone would be inclined to take the morning off, to stick around the house, fueling up on coffee and hot eats, then quietly disperse to get back to work.

Small teams of cooks would form—Lee and Todd would be making fry bread and baked beans. Ethan and Charlotte would be making French toast and fried eggs. Madeline would be making smoothies. Amy and Tess would be making garlicky potatoes with sour cream dip. Jacob would be making a big pile of cooked greens. I might be making mushroom gravy and biscuits. Eventually, all the food would be ready around the same time, and there would be enough to go all around. We'd find ourselves with plates piled to a cartoonish height, and call it a "lumberjack slam."

Potatoes	Sauces and condiments (sour cream, ketchup, pesto)
Paprika	
Eggs	Beans (baked, stewed, or slow-cooked)
Salt	Favorite sausage, cured meat, or smoked fish
Greens of some kind	
Gravy	Pancakes, waffles, or French toast
Onions	Polenta, toast, biscuits, or bagels
	Great coffee

Get a group of the friends you don't see often enough to come over, or get your housemates to pick a time where you can all be together. Or assign elements to each member of your family. You want a table surrounded by people you love with bellies to fill.

Boil some potatoes, then fry them until crisp, dousing with paprika and salt.

Fry or bake eggs in lots of butter.

Wash and dress the greens to your taste, and cook them in a smoking hot wok.

Make the gravy from whatever you have around (mushrooms? sausages? I've made a great one from toasted sunflower seeds . . .), and put it on something (or everything).

Caramelize onions on low for 30 minutes (frying sausages or bacon in the same pan afterwards), then blend them into sour cream with an immersion blender.

Spike ketchup with truffle oil, red pepper flakes, and black pepper.

Heat a can of baked beans, or think about it two days ahead of time and make amazing slow-cooked ones.

Bake something—pastries or biscuits or coffee cake. Fill the kitchen with the scent, fill the room with the anticipation.

Assign someone to constantly be making more coffee.

Spin good records, get too full, enjoy every minute.

breakfast collard greens

Someone in the co-op house once made these perfect collard greens. They wrote suggestions for how to re-create them (with variations) on a piece of scrap paper and stuck it on the range hood with a magnet. The note stayed there, steadily water damaged and splattered with seasonings, long after the author had graduated and moved out. We ordered produce in vast quantities in that house. Whenever someone would be making a lot of pancakes, or trays and trays of roasted potatoes, if I had the time I'd cook like eight bunches of greens down, filling our largest wok, and present them to whoever was milling around the large kitchen.

Collard greens	Onion powder
Oil	White pepper
Syrup of some kind	Nutritional yeast (optional)
Mustard	Salt
Apple cider vinegar	Black pepper
Garlic powder	

Wash the collard greens thoroughly under cold running water. Lay each leaf on a large cutting board, holding it down with one hand and cutting to remove the leaf from its stem. Chop the stems and set aside.

Stack the layers of collard leaves, then roll them up like a treasure map. Take a knife and cut at 1-inch increments, making ribbons. In a big bowl, combine a glug of oil, a squeeze of agave syrup (or maple syrup or Lyle's Golden Syrup or ginger syrup), a blob of mustard, a dash of apple cider vinegar, and some seasonings. These can vary with whatever else you're making for breakfast. The simplest are garlic and onion powders, white pepper, maybe a pinch of nutritional yeast. Whisk with a fork until blended; taste. Add salt and black pepper, and less or more of the other ingredients to taste. When the marinade is good, move the collard ribbons into the bowl, and toss to coat. Let this hang out for a bit while you focus on other parts of the meal.

When you're ready to focus on the greens again, heat a deep cast-iron pan (or alternatively, a wok, but adjust cooking time to be shorter) over medium-high heat. Add a glug of oil. Throw the chopped stems in and fry, seasoning with a bit of salt. When they start to tenderize, turn up the heat and add the dressed leaves. Stir actively while the heat is on high until lots of steam has been released and the greens have really started cooking. Reduce to medium and finish. You can cook them down to Southern-style dark green/brown, or keep them brighter with a little more bite. They will be delicious either way.

SNAPSHOTS OF EATING AND COOKING

I stand in the hallway, unseen, smelling the celery cooking in butter. It's Thanksgiving day. My mother is making the stuffing—my favorite part. Like her cheese sauce, like her crab cakes, like her Jan Hagel (Dutch Almond Christmas cookies), this is the best that food could possibly be.

rye, caraway, black pepper biscuits with mushroom gravy

Biscuits and gravy were my favorite weekend breakfast as a child, both at home and out in the world. A cozy café in Eugene, open since the '60s, is where I had my first excellent mushroom gravy. I still enjoy experiencing everyone's different take on this sure-to-please dish. After years of tasting and experimenting, I have settled on this ideal-to-me version.

Biscuits:

1⅓ cups (171 grams) all-purpose flour, plus more as needed

⅔ cup (85 grams) good northern rye flour

2½ teaspoons baking powder

½ teaspoon baking soda

½ teaspoon salt

Black pepper

2 teaspoons caraway seeds

6 tablespoons (85 grams) cold unsalted butter

¾ cup cultured cream

¾ cup buttermilk or kefir

Gravy:

1 small shallot

Butter

Mushrooms (pretty much any mushroom with an edible stem will work)

3 large cloves garlic

Hungarian paprika

Cayenne pepper

Salt

Black pepper

1 tablespoon all-purpose flour

Whole milk, cream, half-and-half, or buttermilk

Mushroom bouillon or miso (optional)

Apple cider vinegar

To make the biscuits, sift together the flours, baking powder, baking soda, and salt. Biscuit-making is the one time I believe in the benefits of sifting (or at least sorta sifting). You can run all the flour mixture through a fine-mesh sieve if you don't have a sifter. It helps yield a more delicate crumb. Crack loads of black pepper into the dry mix, along with the caraway seeds, and stir with a wooden spoon. Cut the cold butter into pieces and work it in with your fingers.

Put the cultured cream in a measuring cup, pour in the buttermilk and stir to incorporate a little bit. Stir this into the dry ingredients with a wooden spoon until just mixed. Throw some more flour in for ease of handling. Fold the biscuit dough over again and again so you create layers of biscuit to later pull apart. When you've folded it over several times, move the dough to a floured work surface. Roll out with a rolling pin. Fold over one more time. Roll again. Cut to your desired shape (circles? squares? triangles?). Bake at 425 degrees F on a parchment-lined baking sheet for 10 to 12 minutes, or until just starting to color on the top. The bottoms should be quite golden at this point, and you don't want them to go further.

To make the mushroom gravy, chop the shallot finely and add it to a deep saucepan with a large pat of butter. Cook over medium heat until totally softened and starting to color. Remove the stems from the mushrooms, mince them, and set aside. Slice the tops of the mushrooms. Chop the garlic and add to the shallot. When you can smell the garlic, add the minced mushroom stems. Cook until they release moisture and go soft. Add the sliced mushroom tops with another pat of butter. Shake in some Hungarian paprika and a little cayenne pepper. Cover and leave alone for 90 seconds.

Remove the lid and stir actively. The mushrooms should be getting smaller and more tender. Add salt and pepper. Taste some. Is it delicious? If so, great! If not yet, think about adding a dab of mustard or more black pepper.

When this mixture is done, scrape it into a bowl to wait for its return to the pan. In the recently vacated saucepan, set the flame to medium, add another pat of butter and wait for it to melt. Toss in 1 teaspoon of the flour. Ready with a whisk, whisk it into the butter immediately. Add whole milk, cream, half-and-half, or buttermilk. Turn up the heat. Whisk actively until the flour incorporates and the sauce starts to thicken. If you have some mushroom bouillon or miso, a spoonful of that right now is great.

Return the cooked mushrooms, shallot, and garlic to the saucepan. Stir, reduce the heat to low, and cover again. Let the gravy simmer for a while so the mushroom flavor fills out the white sauce. When you are just about to serve, add some splashes of apple cider vinegar. This will really "lift" the whole thing in a beautiful way. If it doesn't have enough kick for you, crack in loads more black pepper, or a touch of chili powder. If you'd like it to be herby, add a small handful of finely chopped herbs just a minute or two before serving.

You should probably also make the breakfast collard greens! To make a lumberjack slam, add potatoes, sour cream, and a shirred egg to your plate and tuck in.

smoked trout breakfast sandwich

A breakfast sandwich for the kind of morning where you make time for sitting outside in the cool air, letting yourself slow down a bit.

---

1 whole smoked trout fillet (salmon works just fine, but trout is cheaper and better here) per 2 to 3 people

Black pepper

Oil

Flaky salt

Favorite baguette-style bread (one with seeds is really nice here)

Best mustard

Cream cheese

Lemon thyme

1 egg per person

Using a fork, carefully remove the trout from its skin, a few bite-size flakes at a time, gathering them in a pile on the cutting board or in a bowl.

Clean the skin of any excess fat that isn't looking good, then place it on a cookie sheet. Brush with oil on both sides, and top with loads of black pepper. Sprinkle with flaky salt. Broil for 3 to 6 minutes with the oven door closed. Listen to the crackle and pop. It will get loud before it is close to done, but as with all things under the broiler, it could burn in a matter of seconds if not closely watched. When the edges start to perk up, take the sheet out, flip the skins over and return to the broiler, this time keeping the door open and watching all the time. When the second side starting to crisp up, but is not blackened by any means, take the sheet out. The trout skin "bacon" will finish crisping in the open air.

Slice the baguette lengthwise. I recommend a baguette because having crust on both sides is essential for the soft filling of the sandwich.

Spread the best mustard in a secret, small layer on the bottom piece of bread. Spread the cream cheese in a thick layer (think bagel shop where they give you almost too much cream cheese) on top of it.

De-stem as many leaves of lemon thyme as you have patience for. Drop as many pieces of smoked trout as you'd like to eat on top of the cream cheese, and press them in a little with a fork to get them to stay on as you bite into your sandwich later. Sprinkle on loads of lemon thyme.

Slice the trout bacon into thin strips.

Fry, poach, bake, or soft-boil an egg to your preferred finish. Cut it in half or drop it in the middle between the pieces of bread. Top with the strips of trout bacon and a generous further cracking of black pepper and sprinkling of flaky salt.

breakfast salad with celery and meyer lemon

The lightest, simplest thing. Works so very well with all manner of breakfasts, especially with pancakes. When we shot it, we also had some of the best soft cheese on the planet—Winnimere from Jasper Hill, Vermont—on the side. The crunch of the celery and bright flavor of the lemon work beautifully with mild, buttery soft cheeses.

Mixed salad greens, including some radicchio

Celery

Lemon juice

Meyer lemon

Parsley

Muscatel or other fancy wine vinegar

Olive oil

Flaky salt

Black pepper

Wash and dry the greens. Cut the celery stalks into lengths about 2½ inches long, then slice into medium-thin strips. Let the celery hang out in ice cold water with a splash of lemon juice in it.

Take your sharpest knife, with the most control, and cut ⅛-inch rounds of Meyer lemon. Then pull the peel off around the edges. Remove the pith in the center, and cut into little triangles.

Tear the parsley off the thicker stems, but keep the thinnest, tender stems towards the top. Make a medium pile on your cutting board. Mix these with the greens in a good bowl.

Dress the salad with some splashes of vinegar to taste, and a little lemon juice to add body to the tangy quality. Add olive oil, also to taste, keeping it pretty light. Toss the dressed greens, add flaky salt and cracked black pepper. Add the celery slices and Meyer lemon and serve.

old world corn cakes with dried blueberries

This recipe was inspired by a high-profile bakery in Portland that serves a perfectly textured cornmeal cookie, featuring the concentrated flavor punch of dried blueberries and an underlying spice from red pepper flakes.

It was also sort of an absurd distillation of the "cook with what you have" idea. Often when making this book, I'd have a set sequence of dishes in mind, shopping and harvesting accordingly. Well, the week before this shoot, I'd helped cook food for a college student retreat, using lots of donated food from businesses around Washington State. Some favorites, which I got to take home a bit of, were dried blueberries and blueberry jam from Bow Hill, an amazing family-owned blueberry farm that has been in operation since 1947. Washington is known for being the most ideal berry-growing area in the world. Bow Hill's products are exquisite, and they sell online!

---

1 cup semolina flour

1 cup medium- or coarsely ground cornmeal or polenta (find an exquisite, extra-special heirloom corn situation from a good farm)

1 teaspoon baking soda

1 teaspoon salt

Big handful of dried blueberries (dry your own or find a small producer that grows good berries and does it well)

Pinch of red pepper flakes

3 eggs, at room temperature

¼ cup brown sugar

2 cups buttermilk

½ cup heavy cream or half-and-half

Oil

Fancy blueberry jam

Mix together the semolina flour, cornmeal, baking soda, salt, fancy dried blueberries, and red pepper flakes.

Beat the eggs with the brown sugar, stir in the buttermilk and heavy cream, then add to the dry ingredients and mix until just combined. Let stand for about 10 minutes.

Heat a skillet that is both thin and good at holding an even temperature. This is so essential for pancakes!

Pour in a small glug of oil and use a spatula to scrape it evenly over the surface of the pan. Wait until it is hot enough to sizzle when a flick of water hits the surface. Take a serving spoon or whatever batter-pouring device you prefer,

(Continued)

and lay the batter down into the pan. Cook one corn cake at first, flipping when the bottom has browned and bubbles have formed over the whole surface. Get into the groove, then do two or three at a time after that.

Serve with the fancy blueberry jam you just happen to have around, or not.

sage omelet

My taste in omelets is heavily influenced by the mid-century English food writer Elizabeth David, who preferred them to be made extremely simply or not at all.

Quite a bit of sage

3 eggs

1 tablespoon dairy: milk is traditional, cream is luxurious, crème fraîche is delightful (I've also used sour cream whisked with a little water)

Butter

Good salt

Canola oil (optional)

Chalky goat's milk slicing cheese (an essential item to be served separately on the side)

This makes one large omelet. Share it with a fellow diner, or make two or three and cut them into wedges to serve a crowd.

Separate the sage leaves into two piles: the prettiest and the others. Chop the others roughly. In a flat, dry heavy skillet, fry the pretty sage leaves over medium heat. If you have a grill spatula (a highly recommended tool: I find I use it for innumerable other things as well as grilling), use it to press the leaves flat into the pan. They will scent the air, then can be turned over and the process repeated. When they start go a bit golden, remove them from the heat and set aside on a plate.

Whisk the eggs with a fork or whisk. When they are most of the way there, add the dairy. Pause to prepare the brown butter–sage filling.

Heat a large portion of butter in a small saucepan. Yes, you are filling your omelet with melted butter. In reality, this is less fatty than filling it with obscene quantities of oozing cheese or hunks of sausage or whatever, and the flavor is sublime. When the butter starts to froth, set a timer for 90 seconds. Let it cook. You'll notice it just starting to brown and filling the air with a nutty scent. Add the handful of chopped sage, reduce to low heat for 30 seconds or so, add a pinch of your best salt, then turn off the heat altogether and set aside.

Heat a pan (those pans with subtly curved edges and very heavy bottoms ideal for omelets really are lovely, but you can make this happen in any old frying pan) over medium. If you have an electric range and thin pans, play it safe and work on medium low. Add a large knob of butter and maybe the tiniest amount of canola oil. When the butter has just started to froth a bit, give the eggs a quick whisking and pour them in, increase the heat to medium-high,

(Continued)

and don't do anything for a good 20 to 30 seconds. When the eggs have taken on the circular shape of the pan, reduce the heat to medium again, and use a spatula to lift the edges, moving uncooked eggs in around them. Agitate the pan so you know the omelet isn't sticking in the center. At this point, add your cooked whole sage leaves, artfully arranged on the still-slightly-raw side of the omelet.

Shake the pan a bit to see if your whole omelet moves in a circle with you. If it does, you're ready to flip. Rather than going for broke, I usually have my spatula in one hand and the pan's handle in the other, lifting the omelet a little with the spatula before flipping with the pan in the other hand. The omelet will near completion almost upon impact, so agitate one more time to make sure it hasn't stuck. Add the brown butter sage sauce and fold the omelet over, revealing the decorative sage leaves. Cook a moment or two more on each side to add a fine golden tint to the outsides.

Serve with fine pieces of a goat's milk slicing cheese on the side. You'll appreciate the taste of the eggs, the sage, and the cheese all the more by pacing out each bite.

smoked oyster hash

This dish happened for the first time in an effort to woo Sofie. I was like "she has great taste, she probably likes oysters." Mostly it was a good move because she loves potatoes.

6 to 9 medium-small potatoes	Stalk of rosemary
Canola oil	1 medium or large cipollini onion (if you can only find small ones, get 2)
Salt	
Flaky salt	Butter
2 small or 1 large bulb of garlic	Sugar
Olive oil	1 tin smoked oysters
	Black pepper

Scrub and rinse the potatoes, chopping them into large bite-size eighths, and place them in a roasting tin. Drizzle with a scant amount of canola oil and season with some fine ordinary salt. Toss to coat and distribute the oil and salt. Preheat the oven to 375 degrees F.

Cut the tops off the garlic bulbs and pull away as much of the papery skins as you can. Drizzle olive oil directly into the exposed tops of the garlic, topping that with the ordinary salt (it mostly serves to draw out the harsh notes from the garlic). Nestle the garlic amongst the potatoes and do a tiny drizzle of olive oil on the potatoes for good measure. Place the roasting tin in the oven and let it go for a good 40 minutes. Make the rest of your breakfast, or any other activity that might take this long, but at 40 minutes take the tin out and add the rosemary. Return to the oven for approximately 20 minutes more.

At this time, peel and thinly slice the onion. Heat a cast-iron pan, put a knob of butter in and add the onion slices. Stir to distribute and sprinkle with pinches of sugar and flaky salt. When they begin cooking in earnest, spread them out on the pan and lower the heat. They will begin to caramelize if you leave them alone a little here, only agitating every so often. When they are almost done, open your tin of oysters. Pour the oystery oil onto the onions in the pan, reduce the heat to low and let them absorb it.

Take the potatoes and garlic out of the oven. When cool enough to handle, pop the garlic from its skins and slice each clove into thirds (or have a friend do it). Place them in a smaller roasting tin or baking dish.

Chop the oysters on a cutting board. Remove the onions from the pan, combine them with the sliced garlic and reserve in a low oven. Drop the oysters in the still-hot oniony pan. They should have enough residual oil to cook with, but if not, add another knob of butter. Sauté, like you would mushrooms, until they become fragrant and barely browned. Remove from the stovetop, add to the onions and garlic, and reserve in the low oven.

Get out a deep-sided, heavy-bottomed pan. Heat it on medium. Chop the cooked potatoes up a bit, retaining some large bites. Melt some butter in the base of the pan and tip in the potatoes. Fry them up just enough to add extra crisp and get them piping hot. Distribute all of the garlic, onions, and oysters. Crack in black pepper. Serve, topped with a good dose of flaky salt, with any number of breakfast dishes.

old bay and garlic potatoes

A breakfast place in my hometown still serves what, to me, are the world's best home fries. I imagine this is the case for everyone and their earliest, favorite breakfast potatoes. This recipe is a subtle nod to those potatoes.

Yukon Gold potatoes	Good salt
Oil	Butter
Old Bay	3 large cloves garlic

Boil water in a medium saucepan or deep-rimmed pan. Wash and slice the potatoes into $1/8$-inch-thick medallions, then cut those in half. Using a spider spoon, lower the potatoes into the water. Cook for about 3 minutes, or until a fork pierces them easily but they don't fall apart. Remove with the spider spoon, drain over the sink for a moment, then set aside.

Dress the potatoes with oil as they cool (it's the same idea as adding the butter and milk to mashed potatoes as they cool so they absorb the fat better), then heat a cast-iron or nonstick pan. Carefully lay pieces of potato into the pan and fry until they start to crisp. Flip. Repeat. You may have to get a system going of removing some from the pan, cooking others, then putting them all together. I usually start a second pan, keep it on low just to keep the potatoes warm and softening through, then keep adding to it as batches finish.

Heat the oven to 200 degrees F. Shake a bunch of Old Bay and salt over the potatoes, toss them, and shake on some more. Place the pan in the oven for about 30 minutes while you prepare the rest of your meal.

At some point before you want to serve, melt some butter in a small saucepan. Peel and chop the garlic cloves. Cook the butter and garlic until fragrant but not brown—a minute or two—then turn off the heat. Add some salt, especially if you're using unsalted butter.

When you are ready to eat, take the potatoes out, drizzle with the garlic butter, toss with more salt, and serve.

sharp cheddar and arugula scones

The basics of this scone recipe were cut out of a newspaper some-time in the 1970s. Aria shared it with me. Her mother had done the clipping, and in their house this was the only true scone. I spent many summers around that house and garden. The copied recipe, in Aria's handwriting, still exists, weathered though it may be, held to my fridge with a magnet.

We evolved it together through years of making it sweet and making it savory. This cheddar and arugula version came after I'd experienced several dissatisfying savory pastries in a row and remembered to create the change instead of waiting around for it to happen on its own.

2½ cups (340 grams) all-purpose flour, plus ½ cup (32 grams) more

1¼ tablespoons baking powder

½ teaspoon fine salt

1 teaspoon black pepper

1½ cups (50 grams) densely packed wild arugula (you can also use parsley or a smaller quantity of rosemary and sage)

5 tablespoons (70 grams) cold unsalted butter

1½ cup (115 grams) grated aged white cheddar cheese, such as Oscar Wilde cheddar from Ireland

2 eggs

¾ cup (170 grams) heavy cream

¼ cup (60 grams) milk

½ teaspoon flaky salt

Combine 2½ cups of the flour, baking powder, fine salt, and cracked black pepper.

Place the arugula, untorn, into a glass measuring cup and pack to 1½ cups. Move out onto a cutting board and tear it into medium-small pieces with your hands into another bowl.

At about this time, preheat the oven to 400 degrees F.

Cut the butter (or rub with your fingers) into the dry mixture. Fold in the grated cheese, stir to coat each piece with the flour, then fold in the arugula.

Beat the eggs in a bowl, then whisk in the cream and milk. Add the wet mixture to the dry mixture. Turn out onto a floured board, knead lightly until smooth, then roll or push out to form a tight circle about 1 inch thick. Using a cookie cutter, food mold, or cup, cut the dough into six large or eight to ten small, rounds. I think a large circle works best for these.

Place the cut scones onto a baking sheet lined with parchment paper. Using a pastry brush, brush the tops of each scone with milk, then add a sprinkle of flaky salt and a cracking of black pepper. Bake for 16 to 24 minutes, depending on size, at 400 degrees F. The point is, after 15 minutes, you must check them very frequently, rotating the pan as you do. Use a flat metal spatula to lift one up and check the bottom. It should be golden a little before the whole scone is done. Take them out and put them back in freely every 2 minutes or so until the scones feels right. They should be just turning golden around the edges, and cheese will have bubbled up here and there.

Let sit approximately 5 minutes before eating. These are delectable on their own, turned into a fried egg sandwich, dipped into soup, or eaten with a cool, crunchy salad.

TEA CAKES

whole grain spice cake with orange, hazelnuts and black tea

During my year off before college, I worked in a doomed but lovely tea house. This is where I first learned a lot of basic culinary skills—I was responsible for making soups, cookies, cakes, and scones as well as running the shop.

I liked all of our teas, but none so much as this pungent orange spice tea. I didn't know where it came from, or how to find it. Then one afternoon I arrived at my high school sweetheart's house out of the rain and wind. She offered me some tea. It was *the* tea! Apparently one of our local natural foods grocers has always carried it. After realizing I had such an affinity for the stuff, she started making me various tea cakes to drink it with. This I did, on many more rainy afternoons spent indoors listening to compilation tapes containing songs by bands like The Smiths and Belle & Sebastian.

This cake is an homage of sorts to that tea and to that time.

⅓ cup (75 grams) whole wheat flour

¼ cup (50 grams) spelt flour

¼ cup (50 grams) all-purpose flour

2½ teaspoons baking powder

¾ teaspoon baking soda

1½ teaspoons ground cardamom

2 tablespoons orange spice black tea (Market Spice orange tea, from Seattle, is highly recommended)

1 cup (100 grams) hazelnuts, ground

½ cup (50 grams) hazelnuts, chopped

3 eggs

¾ cup (175 grams) unsalted butter

½ cup (150 grams) sugar, plus extra for dusting

1 teaspoon vanilla extract

2 Cara cara oranges, 1 zested finely, 1 zested coarsely, both juiced

2 tablespoons, plus 1 teaspoon, orange marmalade

1 tablespoon lemon juice

Whisk the flours, baking powder, baking soda, and cardamom together. Toss in the chopped hazelnuts.

In a clean coffee or spice grinder, grind the black tea to a fine powder, and stir to combine with the ground hazelnuts. Add this mixture to the other dry ingredients, and stir to distribute evenly.

Lightly beat the eggs by hand. In a stand mixer with the whisk attachment, beat the butter and sugar until light and fluffy. Add the eggs to the creamed butter and sugar and briefly beat at a high speed. When smooth and aerated, turn off the mixer and switch to the paddle attachment. Add the vanilla, then turn to "stir," gradually adding the dry ingredients, orange juice and zest, 2 tablespoons of the marmalade, and lemon juice, one bit at a time, alternating (example: a bit of the dry ingredients, some orange juice/zest, some of the marmalade, back to the dry ingredients, and so on) and stopping to scrape down the bowl as needed.

Transfer the batter to a parchment-lined loaf pan, dust with sugar to form a bit of a crust on top, and bake at 350 degrees F for about 60 minutes. Take out the loaf pan, and test with a skewer. Heat the remaining 1 teaspoon marmalade in a microwave for 10 seconds, or use a double boiler, then brush on the top of the cake. Let cool thoroughly. This should keep, wrapped up well, for 3 to 5 days.

rhubarb and white polenta sour cream cake with orange zest, hibiscus, and rosemary

An unusual, exciting, substantial cake that celebrates rhubarb season.

Roasted rhubarb:

9 stalks (330 grams) rhubarb

¼ cup (30 grams) sugar

1½ teaspoons vanilla extract

2½ tablespoons water

Tea cake:

2 cups (320 grams) all-purpose flour, plus more as needed

½ cup (60 grams) whole grain flour mix (or any interesting whole grain flour on its own)

¾ cup (145 grams) white polenta (standard golden will, of course, work too)

¾ cup (75 grams) almond meal (other ground nuts will work too)

¾ cup (175 grams) sugar, plus more for sprinkling

1 heaping teaspoon baking powder

¼ teaspoon salt

¾ cup (150 grams) cold, unsalted butter

About 3 tablespoons orange zest (from about 3 oranges)

About 2 tablespoons rosemary

About 2 tablespoons hibiscus flowers

½ cup (100 grams) sour cream

2 brimming teaspoons honey

2 eggs, at room temperature

Just a little lemon juice

Rose jam or rosewater (optional)

To make the roasted rhubarb, preheat the oven to 350 degrees F. Trim and wash the rhubarb and place in a baking dish where it will fit snugly. Scatter the sugar over the rhubarb, then add the water and vanilla. Move everything around so the sugar is moistened and the vanilla infuses the water. Place in the oven, even if it hasn't reached 350 degrees F yet. Bake for 35 minutes.

To make the tea cake, combine the flours, polenta, almond meal, sugar, baking powder, and salt in a food processor. When they're all there, crumble the butter into smallish pieces and place it in the food processor too. Push the pieces down into the dry mixture, then add more on top, and so on.

Toss in the orange zest. Pound the rosemary briefly with the back of a knife to release the oils, then trim. Add half the hibiscus flowers and chop them with the rosemary. Add both to the food processor as well. Grind the other half of the hibiscus flowers in a clean coffee or spice grinder until you have pink powder (this step can easily be skipped, but it will make the finished cake prettier).

Measure the sour cream into a small bowl, then add the honey, stirring well to incorporate. In a separate bowl, beat the eggs thoroughly with a whisk.

Turn the food processor on for 10 seconds. The dry ingredients should now look like bread crumbs. Dump the contents of the food processor into a larger mixing bowl, then mix in the sour cream–honey mixture with a wooden spoon. Add the lemon juice. Once everything is well distributed, fold in the beaten eggs.

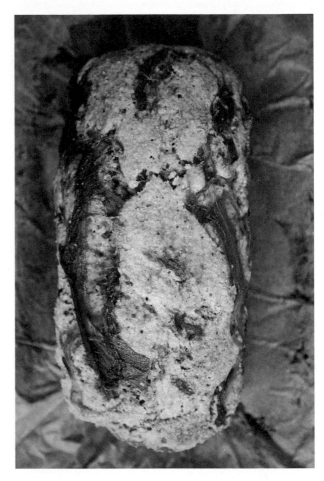

When the rhubarb is done, take it out of the oven and pour over some kind of strainer atop a bowl, using a rubber spatula to get everything out of the pan. Let the rhubarb cool while its juices drain. Add the rhubarb to the mixing bowl in about 3 batches, being careful to mix lightly. You want streaks of pink strands throughout the cake. If it is still not quite wet enough, pour in a little of the reserved rhubarb juice. Conversely, if it seems too wet here, add 1 or 2 tablespoons of flour.

Scrape the batter into a loaf pan lined with parchment (particularly important if you have a metal loaf pan, as rhubarb can do crazy things to metal) and smooth with a rubber spatula. Scatter some sugar on top to help form a crust.

Bake for 60 to 90 minutes at 350 degrees F, depending on your oven, the thickness of your loaf pan, and the precision of your measurements. Test for doneness with a skewer.

In the minutes after removing the cake, pour the remaining rhubarb juice into a small saucepan and turn the heat up to high. Be ready with a spoon. When the liquid starts to bubble furiously, start stirring quickly and carefully. If you have some rose jam or rosewater handy, you can add a little dollop for an extra floral note.

This operation is like making candy: the sugars are getting very hot very fast! When the consistency of the bubbles changes from light and airy to denser and stickier and the liquid has reduced significantly, switch off the heat and lift up the pan. Stir vigorously to get sticky parts along the sides to come down too, then pour over the cake. At this point the top of the cake should have opened and cracked a little bit. Pour the syrup generously into the holes. After about 10 minutes, remove from the loaf pan and let cool completely before serving.

blackberry and blue cornmeal cake with lemon verbena

This is the summer sister cake to the Rhubarb and White Polenta Sour Cream Cake (page 220).

This came about on a summer morning, beginning with the discovery of a few blackberry brambles that had survived my winter attempt to hack away all traces of them. I had just finished watering the garden and was headed back to the shed when a bramble snagged my shirt. They had reached up over the shed, through some trees, and were hanging down at my eye level. The berries were abundant, plump, juicy, and largely seedless. I felt compelled to make something to celebrate them.

About 2 cups (300 grams) all-purpose flour

1 cup (175 grams) blue cornmeal ¾ cup (75 grams) almond meal, plus more for sprinkling

¾ cup (175 grams) sugar, plus more for sprinkling

1 teaspoon baking powder

½ teaspoon cream of tartar

¼ teaspoon salt

1½ sticks (150 grams) cold unsalted butter

3 tablespoons black sesame seeds

¾ cup (100 grams) sour cream

Honey

Lemon verbena or lemon thyme

1 tart green summer apple

Lemon juice

2 eggs, at room temperature

1 pint blackberries: about 12 for the cake, and about 12 for the sauce (minus the berries you'll eat while mixing the batter)

1 teaspoon ginger preserves

Drop the cornmeal, flour, almond meal, sugar, baking powder, cream of tartar, and salt into the food processor. Cut and crumble the butter into small pieces, pushing them down into the dry mix, adding more on top, and so on.

Toast a thin layer of black sesame seeds in a dry pan over medium heat. When they start to smell a little toasty, tip them into the food processor. Turn the processor on for 10 seconds. The dry ingredients should now look like bread crumbs.

Measure the sour cream into a small bowl, then add a spoonful of honey, stirring well to incorporate. Chop the lemon verbena. Grate the apple with the coarse side of a grater. Sprinkle with lemon juice.

Beat the eggs thoroughly with a whisk.

Dump the contents of the food processor into a larger mixing bowl, then stir in the sour cream mixture with a wooden spoon. Add the grated apple and lemon verbena. Once everything is well distributed, fold in the beaten eggs.

Add half of the blackberries, being careful now to mix gently.

Scrape the batter into a loaf pan lined with parchment paper and smooth with a rubber spatula. Scatter some sugar and almond meal on top. Press a few choice berries into the top, reserving a few more to garnish at the end.

Bake at 375 degrees F for 60 to 90 minutes, depending on your oven, the thickness of your loaf pan, and the precision of your measurements. Test for doneness with a skewer.

While the cake is in the oven, make the blackberry syrup. Drop the remaining berries into a heavy-bottomed skillet, followed by the ginger preserves, 1 teaspoon honey, and 1 teaspoon lemon juice. Cook over medium heat until the berries are bursting and bubbling around the edges. Move them to a fine-mesh sieve set over a bowl. Set a heavy object as close to the width of your sieve as you can find on top and smash those berries! Let the juice trickle down, and press out any last pieces. Return the juice to the pan and cook down over medium-high heat until it is just starting to thicken.

Once done, remove the tea cake from the loaf pan. Drizzle with blackberry syrup about 10 minutes later, and let cool completely before serving. Great with iced black tea or cold brew coffee.

apple and blanched almond cake

This cake came about during the three-week window where I could find a favorite old English variety of apple called Ashmead's Kernel. This apple has an extremely lemony quality to it and a beautifully pale-green matte skin. It works very well in pies and cakes. The flesh turns smooth rather than grainy as it cooks. I knew I wanted to make something with Ashmead's Kernel.

But before the whole idea had formulated, I was blanching almonds. I had bought too many at the grocery store's recent bulk blowout sale. I stood at the kitchen sink, running cold water and popping them out of their skins. I had one overripe pear in a paper bag. The previous weekend, I'd made a spelt tea cake from *Tartine Book No. 3* by Chad Robertson. Suddenly, it clicked: blanched almonds, spelt, whole wheat, tart apples, the pear secretly smashed up into the wet ingredients adding fruit-sweetness, then a brown sugar and honey glaze.

I made the cake, using the vintage Bennington Potters loaf pan my friend Holly gave me for the first time. I went to college where these are made, so it sparked the sentimental flame that is needed, I think, for quality baked goods.

About 1½ cups or ½ pound (220 grams) raw almonds	Scant 2 tablespoons (25 grams) whole wheat flour
¾ cup (175 grams) unsalted butter	2½ teaspoons baking powder
½ cup (125 grams) sugar	¾ teaspoon baking soda
3 eggs	2 small exquisite, tart apples
1 very ripe medium to large pear	Lemon juice
Scant ½ cup (100 grams) whole wheat flour	Brown sugar
Scant ¼ cup (50 grams) spelt flour	Honey

Boil some water and pour it over the almonds set out in a bowl. Wait about 90 seconds, then drain and run under cold water. Peel off the skins, chop the almonds in half, and set aside.

Mix the butter and sugar in a stand mixer until fluffy and creamy. Crack the eggs into a bowl and beat lightly with a fork. Incorporate into the butter and sugar with the mixer on low.

Stem, seed, and chop the whole pear, then add it the wet mixture.

In a separate bowl, mix the flours, baking powder, and baking soda.

Slice the apples thinly, about ¼ inch thick. Put slices in a bowl and squeeze/pour some lemon juice over them. Add a generous pinch of brown sugar or a spoonful of honey.

Add the dry ingredients to the butter-sugar mixture one bit at a time, pausing to scrape down the bowl. When the mixture is mostly complete, add the blanched almonds and the apples, reserving some of each for the top. Scrape the entire thing into a parchment-lined loaf pan.

Decorate the top with almonds and fanned-out apples. Sprinkle with brown sugar and a drizzle of honey. Bake at 375 degrees F for 60 minutes. Start checking at around 50 minutes. It may need to bake for closer to 70 minutes, as it really depends on the thickness of your pan. Pull the cake out of the loaf pan after about 10 minutes. Let it rest for at least another 10 minutes. Serve warm, outside if possible, with tea.

SWEETS

pulla (finnish cardamom pastry)

This is a pastry that I fell in love with at the world-class Heart Coffee here in Portland. Their original location is a few blocks from the school where I used to teach. The year after they opened I would get up super early and arrive at seven, to sit with a book and eat pulla with a coffee before work. I learned to make them myself after scrounging through Aria's mom's old Finnish baking books, trying all the variations, then coming up with my own version, inspired by Heart's.

The explosion of flavor from the cardamom pods, surrounded by rich pastry, then chased by bright, light-roasted coffee is an experience you must have!

Pastry dough:

2 teaspoons active dry yeast

¼ cup (60 milliliters) warm water

1 cup (235 milliliters) milk

1½ teaspoons ground cardamom

½ cup (100 grams) sugar

½ teaspoon salt

1 egg plus 1 egg yolk

6 tablespoons unsalted butter, very soft

4½ cups (575 grams) all-purpose flour

Filling:

¼ or ⅓ (60 milliliters or 80 milliliters) cup milk, plus more for brushing

2 to 3 tablespoons muscovado or brown sugar

2 tablespoons butter, very soft

1 tablespoon cardamom seeds (shelled from their pods)

1 teaspoon ground cinnamon

½ teaspoon ground cloves

½ teaspoon ground cardamom

Topping:

Rock or pearl sugar of some kind

Demerara sugar, shaved almonds, oats, or poppy seeds

Dissolve the yeast in the warm water. On the stove, heat the milk until just scalded. Mix in the ground cardamom. Immediately take the pan outside and let the milk cool a little, taking in the amazing smell as the cardamom-scented steam rises up into the air.

Bring it back inside and combine the warm milk with the yeast and water. Let this sit for 7 minutes to proof. Add the sugar, salt, egg and egg yolk, and butter. Beat or blend to integrate. Add the flour, 1 cup at a time, mixing with a wooden spoon. Get the dough out and knead it, adding more flour as needed, for about 10 minutes. Get to the point where the dough is "smooth as a baby's bottom" and bounces back when you punch it down.

Let the dough rest and rise in the oven at 85 degrees F to 100 degrees F for 1 hour, covered with a hot wet dish towel. To get the oven to the right temperature, set it to its lowest setting (often 170 degrees F), keep it on for 5 to 10 minutes, then turn it off. Halfway through the rising time, to keep the temperature steady, place a metal bowl filled with boiling water in the oven. The steam will raise the ambient temperature.

Separate the dough into two balls (punch these down and knead again), then roll out into two thin rectangles.

Combine all the ingredients for the filling in a bowl. Spread the filling mixture evenly over one dough rectangle. Place the second rectangle on top, then roll into a log. Cut the log into triangular pieces. This is best done with a dough scraper or a serrated knife. Place each piece, pressing down in the center to open up the sides, on a parchment-lined baking sheet. Brush with milk and sprinkle with the toppings.

Bake at 400 degrees F for 15 to 20 or minutes, until starting to turn golden.

bitter chocolate cake

I only really love chocolate when it tastes like this: face-smackingly intense, bright, and beautiful, like the best coffee. (I also love old-fashioned chocolate milkshakes, but that's a whole other zone.)

⅔ cup (145 grams) unsalted butter

¼ cup (60 grams) sugar

1 egg

1½ cups (140 grams) unsweetened cocoa powder

1½ cups (140 grams) almond meal

1 tablespoon brown sugar

2 teaspoons cream of tartar

1 teaspoon baking powder

⅔ cup (260 grams) sour cream

1 tablespoon coffee liqueur

About ½ a bar of good, dark, standard-size (about 1.75 ounces) chocolate

Demerara sugar

Flaky salt

Cream the butter and sugar together in a stand mixer at a high speed with the whisk attachment, until quite light and fluffy. Add the egg, scrape down the sides with a rubber spatula, shake out the whisk and replace with the paddle attachment. Then beat on low.

In a separate bowl, combine the cocoa powder, almond meal, brown sugar, cream of tartar, and baking powder. Tip them into the stand mixer bowl. Mix on medium-low until they start to incorporate. Stop, add all of the sour cream, and continue. The batter should be wet enough now, and just getting to a good, smooth consistency. Increase the mixing speed. Add the coffee liqueur. When the batter is smooth and a fair amount of air has gotten into it, turn off the mixer.

Grease a small baking dish; this cake can be made rectangular "brownie" style or circular, "nice cake" style. I have these great small cake pans with a tool built in that helps you lift them out of the pan without breaking or sticking. Grease whatever pan you are using, or line with parchment paper.

Scrape the batter into the pan and smooth the top with a rubber spatula. Break your chocolate into good-looking pieces and stick them on the surface of the cake. Sprinkle with demerara sugar, then flaky salt.

Bake at 325 degrees F for approximately 45 minutes. Check at about 35 minutes. The top should have firmed up and a toothpick inserted should come out swiftly, if not entirely clean.

This intense cake needs to be accompanied by coffee or dessert wine or both (one following the other, over the course of one slice, is pretty euphoric).

walnut and dried fig coffee cake

For this recipe, we just happened to have some leftover pear-poaching liquid with white wine and saffron from a Secret Restaurant dinner the day before. I don't expect anyone to have pear-poaching liquid with white wine and saffron just hanging around. If you do, hey! Great! If not, be resourceful.

A big handful of dried figs	½ cup (120 milliliters) milk
Soaking liquid, such as apple or pear juice, brandy, rum, or cognac	1 tablespoon honey, plus more for drizzling
	1 teaspoon vanilla extract
2 cups (200 grams) raw walnuts	1 cup (160 grams) whole wheat flour
1 stick (115 grams) unsalted butter	1½ teaspoons baking powder
¼ cup (100 grams) sugar	1 larger handful of almond meal
2 eggs	1 tablespoon brown sugar

Soak the figs in the liquid of your choosing. Once the figs are rehydrated, drain and chop them.

Toast the walnuts in a 375-degree-F oven for 10 minutes, or until just starting to get quite fragrant. Let cool and reserve.

Cream the butter and sugar together in a stand mixer until golden and fluffy. Reduce the speed to low, crack in the eggs, and add the milk, honey, and vanilla.

Mix the flour and baking powder in a separate bowl and add them slowly to the wet mixture. Then add the chopped rehydrated figs.

Roughly chop the walnuts, making sure to end up with both small and nearly whole pieces. When you've reached ideal wet-ish cake batter consistency, add most of the walnuts, saving some bigger pieces for the top.

Spread the batter into a cake pan lined with parchment paper. Press the extra walnuts into the top of the cake. Drizzle some honey over it in a crisscross pattern. Shake a bunch of almond meal over the honey, then sprinkle on the brown sugar.

Bake at 375 degrees F for 35 to 40 minutes, or until a fork or skewer comes out clean and the top has a nice, almost-crisp quality.

black pepper cheesecake

This is a great thing to make for those gloomy spring days when the strawberries have just come. Sometimes your belly just desires something decadent and a glass of wine. Do yourself a favor: buy a bottle of Beaujolais and a pint of strawberries and make this cheesecake. Made in an unusual vessel for a cheesecake—the loaf pan—this recipe leaves one with a more sensible quantity of such a decadent dessert.

Crust:

1 stick (113 grams) butter, softened

¼ cup (50 grams) brown sugar

1 cup (125 grams) all-purpose flour

Filling:

½ cup (about 100 milliliters) European-style yogurt

½ cup (about 50 milliliters) whole milk or heavy cream

⅔ cup (75 grams) powdered sugar

1 pound (16 ounces/470 grams) or about 2 cups cream cheese

Black pepper

Zest from 1 lemon

Strawberry-Beaujolais Compote (recipe follows)

For the crust, cream the butter with the brown sugar, then add the flour, working until fully incorporated. It will become the most exquisite cookie dough.

Line a loaf pan with parchment paper and press the dough into the bottom of the pan. It will be nearly ½ inch thick. Spread the top smooth with a tool of some kind and bake at 350 degrees F for 25 to 35 minutes. It should start to smell slightly toasty, but be careful, there is a small burn threshold with shortbread, even one this thick. Remove from the oven and cool completely. This can be done a day or two in advance, as shortbread keeps very well.

For the filling, place the yogurt and milk in a metal bowl and whisk in the powdered sugar until fluffy with air. If using heavy cream, it will start to thicken—you want to stop before it does too much. (I do this in a stand mixer with the whisk attachment. Using a hand mixer or hand beater also works well. The point is fast and furious! You want a luxuriously smooth cheesecake.)

Add the cream cheese, lemon zest, and black pepper. The simplest way of measuring the quantity of black pepper is to crack a heavy dusting over the bowl, mix it in, and repeat three times. Now flecks of black pepper should be visible throughout the mixture.

(Continued)

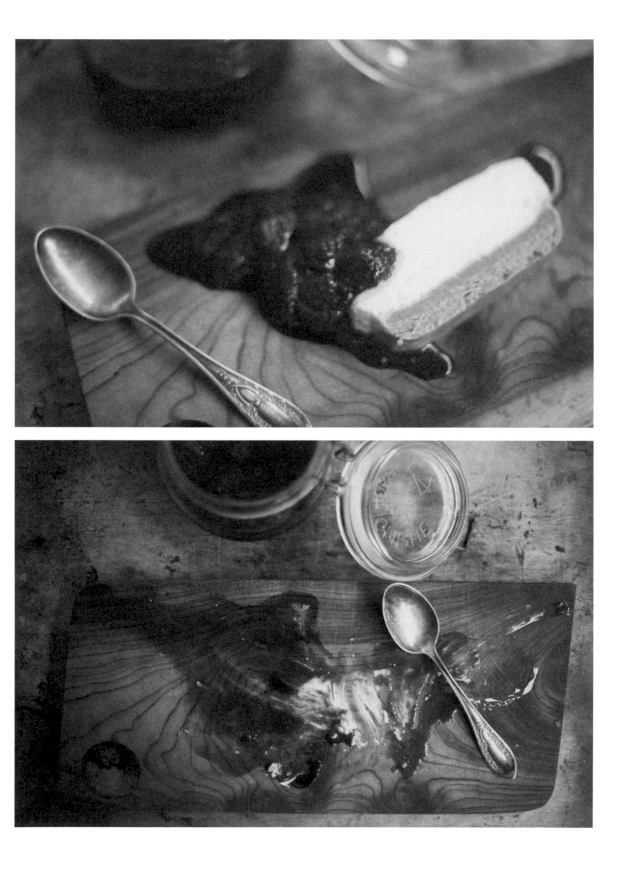

Taste the mixture to see if it is peppery enough for you. Scrape it into the loaf pan and smooth the top. Cover and chill for at least 6, if not 24, hours.

To serve, lift the cake out of the loaf pan gently and unwrap. Pour boiling water over a sharp knife, then slice with the hot knife, laying the pieces down on plates gently.

Serve with the compote.

STRAWBERRY-BEAUJOLAIS COMPOTE

1 pint (400 grams) ripe and winey strawberries

¼ cup (50 grams) sugar

2 teaspoons lemon juice

Scant ½ cup (100 milliliters) Beaujolais wine

Slice the tops off of your strawberries, and slice the larger ones in halves or quarters so all the pieces are around the same size.

Put the strawberries in a medium saucepan with the sugar and lemon juice. Turn the heat to medium and stir. When the temperature has risen and they are starting to bubble and froth, turn the heat down to medium-low. Skim off the froth. Repeat, cooking for 10 to 15 minutes, or until the juices have reduced a bit. Raise the heat to medium again and add the wine. Stir to incorporate, then turn back down to medium-low. Cook for 5 minutes more, skimming the froth off once again.

Pour into a good-looking jar and use within 3 days. This is not meant to keep! To illustrate this point, it is shown on the previous page in an old French hermetically sealing jar I got at a garage sale for 25 cents and haven't ever gotten around to finding a replacement seal for.

rhubarb, raspberry, and redcurrant crumble

My garden has a rhubarb hill, long-established raspberry canes, and a redcurrant bush. One time, around the beginning of July, when all three were bountiful and I had these leftover, half-broken Italian wafer cookies lying around, this crumble materialized. It felt as if it was suggested by the people who had planted the garden long ago and by my friend who forgot the cookies at the event she had brought them to.

I hope you can come to a similar equation with whatever fruit you have access to, and either make this crumble or one in the same spirit. Really, with a crumble, precise measurements are unnecessary. Just choose a dish you want to make it in and include enough fruit to fill it.

---

4 or 5 stalks rhubarb

2 large handfuls of raspberries

Sugar

A healthy drizzle of Lyle's Golden Syrup, honey, agave, or something like that

1 stick (100 grams) unsalted butter, plus more as needed

Oats

All-purpose flour

Almond meal or almonds you grind yourself

A few pizzelles (Italian wafer cookies), if you can get your hands on them

A handful of redcurrants, top and tailed

Cut, wash, and trim the rhubarb. If you are making this recipe at the height of the season, when all three of these fruits are fresh, your rhubarb has likely been around for a while. If the outside is tough, peel it with a vegetable peeler. Cut the rhubarb into pieces about 4 inches long and put in your baking dish.

Take a handful of raspberries and crush them in your hand. Scrape the berries off with a rubber spatula and onto the rhubarb. Scatter about a ¼ cup sugar around the edges and on top. Drizzle the syrup on as well. Tuck in small pieces of butter, about one-sixth of the stick.

In a food processor add the remaining butter (cut into pieces), sugar, oats, flour, almond meal, and Pizzelles (reserving one to crumble on top). Pulse a few times until the butter is cut up and pebbles have formed. Add 1 or 2 tablespoons of cold water and shake the bowl of the food processor until pebbles really form.

(Continued)

Spread the crumble mixture over the fruit. Take the second handful of raspberries and scatter them throughout the crumble. This will cause them to burst appetizingly into the crust. Crack the final pizzelle over the top of the crumble.

Bake at 350 degrees F for 50 minutes.

If the crumble isn't browning, take another slice of butter and break it up over the top. Return the pan to the oven for 10 to 15 more minutes, until the rhubarb has started to bubble up around the edges.

Drop the raw redcurrants around the crisped-up pizzelle pieces. Serve with extra sugar at the table. Keeping the crumble nice and tart but having the option to sweeten up some bites is a more enjoyable eating experience than all tart or all sweet. Pretend you are a child at the breakfast table, adding sugar to the top of a cut grapefruit.

almond cake with tart fruit and elderflowers

I'll eat any almond cake that comes my way. My favorite breakfast café, a short walk from my house, does a nearly perfect one. That doesn't stop me from making them whenever I have the inclination and the ingredients around.

This is particularly delicious eaten in the grass with flowery tea, rosé, or madeira.

¾ stick (75 grams) unsalted butter

¼ cup (58 grams) sugar, plus more for sprinkling

2 eggs

½ cup plus 1 tablespoon (150 milliliters) heavy cream or half-and-half

⅛ teaspoon almond extract (the tiniest whiff on the wind, rather than overpowering and boozy)

1 teaspoon elderflower liqueur (optional)

1¾ cups (175 grams) almond meal

A generous ½ cup (75 grams) all-purpose flour, plus more as needed

1 teaspoon baking powder

½ teaspoon cream of tartar

A few cut fronds of fresh elderflowers, or 1 scoop of dried

White, red, or black currants; white or red grapes; gooseberries; or any tart summer berry

Powdered sugar

(*Continued*)

Cream the butter and sugar in a stand mixer fitted with the whisk attachment. Add the eggs and mix on low until yellow and frothy. Add about half of the cream and the almond extract. If you have elderflower liqueur around, a teaspoon here would not go amiss.

Whisk mix the almond meal, flour, baking powder, and cream of tartar in a separate bowl, then add gradually add to the mixer on low.

When batter is mixed but seems slightly too thick, add the second half of the cream, then half of the elderflowers. Follow this, using your best judgment to achieve ideal cake batter texture, with some additional all-purpose flour. You want the batter to be quite moist but not so much so that it will immediately run off the mixing spoon.

Scrape the mixture into a smallish parchment-lined cake pan. Press the white currants or other tart fruit into the top of the cake. Sprinkle with some sugar (to help form a crust on the top), then bake at 375 degrees F for 30 to 40 minutes. Let cool completely, then top with powdered sugar and the rest of the elderflowers.

SNAPSHOTS OF EATING AND COOKING

The elderly pastry chef at the restaurant owned by my friend's dad is slipping us samples as we stand around the kitchen, the warm ovens and frantic pace a beautiful blur.

During a bite of this cake, one should experience the following: the dense but open crumb, a full almond flavor, a not-too-sweet then bright zing from a currant or two, a kiss of super sweetness from the powdered sugar, and the perfume of flowers floating above it all.

apricots and white currants with elderflower

Succulent summer fruit with floral liqueur. Easy and delicious.

Apricots, as many as you like

White currants, as many as you like, or seedless white wine grapes or other tart fruit

St. Germain or other elderflower liqueur

Sugar (optional)

Vanilla ice cream, for serving

Shortbread cookies, for serving (see Figgy Shortbreads, page 244)

Cut the apricots into halves and remove the pits. Clean and de-stem the currants.

Arrange the apricots in a baking dish, then scatter with the currants. Pour a generous ½ cup elderflower liqueur over the fruit. If this still doesn't seem like enough, go big with the elderflower liqueur, or add a ¼ cup water and a few teaspoons of sugar.

Roast at 375 degrees F for 45 to 60 minutes. The apricots and currants should release some of their juices, which will be flavored by the liqueur. Remove the fruit and juices from the pan and put them into a jar. Let this chill completely in the fridge. Serve with the most luscious vanilla ice cream you can find, and maybe buttery shortbread cookies.

blueberry tart with lemon curd

A man Asher and Marit knew brought us a giant flat of low-bush wild Maine blueberries he had picked. They asked for wild blueberry pie. I worked on the filling and the lemon curd late into the night before the big dinner, long after my hosts had gone to bed.

For ease of planning, simply make the lemon curd separately (the best recipe in the world, to me, is Nigel Slater's "a couple pots of lemon curd" from *Notes from the Larder*) ahead of time.

Basic pie dough:

1 stick (113 grams) unsalted butter

1½ cups (200 grams) all-purpose flour

Good salt

Lemon thyme, if you have any

1 to 2 tablespoons sour cream or crème fraîche, if you happen to have any around

5 to 6 tablespoons (75 to 90 milliliters) ice water

Pie Filling:

1 to 2 pounds blueberries

Sugar

3 to 5 tablespoons lemon juice

Golden sugar

Your favorite lemon curd, for serving

For the crust, freeze the butter, or at least put it in the freezer for a while before starting. In a food processor or large bowl, combine the flour and a pinch of good salt. Cut the butter into small pieces, crumbling as you go, and drop them in with the flour. Blitz four or five times until the mixture is quite pebbly. Add the lemon thyme, if you're into that, and move the mixture to a mixing bowl. Mix in the sour cream or crème fraîche.

Add the ice water 1 tablespoon at a time, incorporating with a wooden spoon. When you can form the dough into a ball, do so, roll it up in plastic wrap, and refrigerate for 1 hour. After the chilling stage, roll it out into a wide, rustic octagon. Freeze again, sitting on a parchment-lined flat baking sheet while you make the filling.

For the filling, wash the blueberries and set aside a quarter of them. Add the rest to a saucepan with a generous scattering of sugar. Soak the sugar with the lemon juice. Cook over medium heat. The blueberries will intensify in color, then start to burst. At this stage, remove from the heat and strain into a bowl set under a fine-mesh sieve. Press to encourage as much of the juice to go through as possible. Reserve the cooked berries.

Take the collected juice, return it to the saucepan, and bring to a boil, stirring constantly. It will begin to thicken and stick to the sides. When it begins to resemble syrup, turn off the heat and return the cooked berries to the mixture. Taste and add more sugar or lemon juice as desired for a sweeter or more tart filling. You've made a sure-to-not-be-runny filling. Let it cool.

Preheat the oven to 375 degrees F. When the filling has cooled completely, take out the frozen crust. Spread the filling in a circle in the center. Dump in the reserved fresh blueberries, spreading them around and pressing in with your fingers. This will create a luscious, multidimensional blueberry experience. Let the edges of the crust defrost until they are just ready to be folded over, then do so. Brush the edges with water, then sprinkle with your nicest golden sugar. Put the pie in the oven immediately.

Start watching it after 30 minutes. You want the crust to start going golden, but you really don't want the blueberries to overcook.

When the pie is done and cooled, dollop generously with lemon curd. This goes exquisitely well served with black cups of Ethiopian coffees that often have blueberry and lemon notes in their flavor profiles.

figgy shortbreads

These are very versatile shortbreads that go well with simple fruit desserts. The recipe can be adapted to suit any dried fruit. Apricots, pears, and cranberries work particularly well.

---

1 cup (250 grams) chilled unsalted butter

½ cup (100 grams) sugar

½ teaspoon almond extract

1½ cups (225 grams) all-purpose flour

½ cup (60 grams) semolina flour

A handful of chopped dried figs

Black pepper

Cream the butter, sugar, and almond extract with a fork and some patience or a stand mixer fitted with the paddle attachment. Work in the flours gradually, then add the dried figs and black pepper. Chill the dough for 20 minutes in the freezer or 1 hour in the fridge. You can also freeze it, thaw it, and bake them later.

When you roll the dough out about ¼ inch thick, the figs should flatten perfectly. Cut the dough into shapes with a cookie cutter or a cup upside down and table knife. Move them with a thin metal spatula to a parchment-lined baking sheet.

Bake at 325 degrees F for 10 to 15 minutes, or until just starting to go golden. Remove to a cooling rack and repeat until they've all been baked and cooled.

fresh fig tart

This tart features late-summer figs, dripping with juice, on top of tangy cheese and a flaky herb crust. Try eating this outside, right out of your hands, before sunset and washing it down with sparkling wine.

Basic pie dough (from Blueberry Tart with Lemon Curd on page 242), with an herb like lemon thyme or rosemary, for intrigue

Some delicious, simple, high-quality chèvre

A drop or two of milk, yogurt, or heavy cream

Powdered sugar

Fresh, ripe figs

Honey

Sparkling wine

Roll the dough out into circles to fit medium-small tart pans or baking vessels. This can work as a large tart but is better as a smaller "sharing" size (or do it in muffin tins as tartlets). Bake at 375 degrees F for 15 to 25 minutes, depending on their size, with pie weights or whatever method you like best to keep the shell intact. Let cool, then remove from the pan(s).

In a bowl, whip the chèvre with your drop or two of milk and a pinch (really, only a pinch) of powdered sugar.

Spread the chèvre mixture gently into the baked shell(s), being careful not to break it/them.

Take the tops off of the figs, then open them up like flowers with your hands. When you have two halves, take a knife and quarter them. Set the fig pieces attractively and snugly next to each other on top of the creamy cheese. Drizzle with honey and serve with sparkling wine.

whiskey ginger pears

An easy, affordable, fantastic dessert that can cook alongside the preparations for the rest of a meal.

Notes on your choice of ingredients:

Pears a few days from syrupy ripeness are ideal for this, and we are teasing them into that state by cooking them this way.

Rye whiskey is particularly nice here. George Dickel Rye is quite good, made in the same place as Bulleit, just with a different recipe and ten dollars cheaper. You can, of course, use whatever whiskey you might have around.

Ginger People Ginger Syrup is a fantastic product. You could make it yourself but it wouldn't be as delicious or affordable (a plentiful bottle is four dollars).

---

1 pear per person (Comice are especially nice)

Whiskey

Ginger syrup

A few lemon slices per person

Slice your pears in half down the center, removing the seeds and pithy core with a small pointy spoon or paring knife.

Find a baking dish that your halved pears will fit snugly into.

Add a shot of whiskey per pear, 1 teaspoon water per pear, and 1 teaspoon ginger syrup per pear.

Swish the dish around so the whiskey, water and syrup mix. Roll the pears around in the mixture, or spoon it over them a few times. Have them lying cut side down at first. Squeeze over some of your lemon slices and tuck them in around the edges.

Bake at 350 degrees F for 1 hour or so. Take the pan out halfway through, turn the pears over, and baste them in the pan juices, baking cut-side up for the remaining time.

To serve, move two halves of pear per person to small bowls, spooning over plenty of the juices as you go. Squeeze out the last of the lemon slices on top of each serving.

russet / rye apple pie

There is a stand at the Portland Farmers Market called Old World Apples. They have an orchard planted with innumerable heirloom varieties, but only a handful of trees each. I go nearly every week in the fall. Russet apples, in early November, are a favorite. This pie happened for the first time on a quiet evening alone, when I had a fresh bag of rye flour and a bowl of russet apples on the counter.

Rye crust:

1 stick (113 grams) unsalted butter

1 cup (120 grams) all-purpose flour

A generous ½ cup (70 to 80 grams) dark northern rye flour

½ teaspoon salt

5 to 8 teaspoons (100 milliliters) ice water

Filling:

5 apples, preferably heirloom (if it's November and you can find Brown Russets, those are the ones!), or 5 Bosc pears (these have the matte warm brown skin, like the russet apples—if you use these instead, add a lot of extra lemon juice as they don't have the tartness of the apples)

2 tablespoons unsalted butter

About 1½ tablespoons lemon juice

2 tablespoons apple cider

1 heaping tablespoon brown sugar

½ teaspoon vanilla extract

To make the crust, cut the stick of butter into small pieces and put it in the freezer a bit before you are going to make the dough. After 20 minutes or so, place the flours, salt, and frozen butter into a food processor and blitz. Many quality pie recipes extoll on the fine pleasures of rubbing the butter in with your hands. I agree, but it is easier to get perfect flaky crust by forming pebbles of cold butter, and this is much more achievable in the food processor. After blitzing for 30 seconds or so, stop, check, then pulse some more. Add 2 teaspoons of the ice water, pulse again, and move the dough to a bowl.

Continue to add ice water, 1 teaspoon at a time, until the dough balls up. Roll the dough ball in flour, wrap in plastic wrap, then chill in the fridge for 45 to 60 minutes.

To make the filling, slice the apples: quarter them, then slice lengthways to get two or three thin pieces out of each quarter. Halfway through

the cutting, heat a wide-rimmed pan over medium and melt the butter in it. Add the apples you've chopped, toss with lemon juice, and repeat until all the apples are in the pan. Add the apple cider and cook, stirring frequently. When the apples begin to soften but are still quite underdone, add the brown sugar and vanilla, tossing actively to distribute and perfume the apples. When they get to the next stage of tenderness, but still aren't done, turn off the heat and cover the pan. The residual heat will steam the apples. After 5 minutes or so, take off the lid and set the pan out to cool.

Take a break. Tend the garden, empty the dish drainer, hang up some laundry.

Retrieve the dough from the fridge and roll it out on a lightly floured work surface. When it is a rustic circle, bigger than your pie pan, lift it into the pie pan. If you're using a glass or ceramic dish, there is no need for parchment, but if it's a thin pan, maybe use some just in case. Press the dough into the pan, but leave the edges hanging off. Put it in the freezer.

Once the filling is room temperature and/or the dough has been freezing for 5 to 8 minutes, take out the crust, pour the filling into the center, fold the edges over, and bake at 425 degrees F for 10 minutes. Rotate the pan, then reduce the heat to 375 degrees F and bake for 35 minutes. Rotate the pan, then reduce the heat to 325 degrees F and bake for 25 minutes to finish.

When the crust is golden on the bottom and going golden around the top, take the pie out to cool a bit before eating. This is excellent served hot with ice cream, room temperature with cheddar as a "meal," or leftover with coffee as breakfast.

THANK YOU

Peter and Kate

We would like to thank our friends and family for all their love and support throughout the making of this book. Especially Brent and Terressa Schweiter, this project could not have been possible without your encouragement and continued belief in our work. We love you.

And finally to Andrew, thank you for asking, and for filling our nights with delicious food and pushing on to create this cookbook and the recipes inside its pages.

Andrew

Thanks to Peter and Kate Schweitzer, for saying yes and executing it beautifully.

To all the editors and recipe testers. You made it work!

To Lucas Winiarski, for the years in the kitchen together (and the hallways of school before that).

To Russell Melia, always and forever.

To Sofie Sherman-Burton, for actually everything.

To my parents,
Robert and Carrol Barton—
    I love you!

FOR THE INFLUENCE, INSPIRATION, AND SUPPORT

Mary Sherman and
    Vern Nelson
Sheila Ryskamp
Dave and Susan Morgan
Cher Mikkola

My roommates, past and
    present, for living with
    this thing in production:
Katie Savastano
Marta King
Allie Cislo

College Homies, for
    the love, help, and
    inspiration:

Emma Morehouse
Holly Meyers
Zoe Donnellycolt
The Liberal Arts Bros:
Asher Woodworth
Trevor Wilson
Hamilton Poe
Nate Luce

Nolan Calisch
Chris Seigel

Kellen Hopfner

Joshua James Amberson

*Especially supportive parents of
students of mine:*
Holly Telerant and
    Rob Blau
Jennifer Marfori and
    Reese Lord
Andy and Lisa Prince
David Sussman and Tonya
    Wolfersperger
Cynthia Tuan
Sue Kim and
    Dylan Magierek
Beth and Ben Byers

CREDITS

Original project editor:
Delphine Bedient

Assistant editors:
Kate Schweitzer
Sofie Sherman-Burton
Alleson Goldfinger

Recipe testers/dear friends:
Anna Kariel
Jodi Geren
Alleson Goldfinger
Holly Meyers
Erin Perry
Al Pomper
Emily Tareila
Trevor Wilson
Asher Woodworth

You are a strong influence,
    thank you:

(Portland)
Kevin Gibson
John Taboada
Sarah Minnick
Kim Boyce

(England)
Nigel Slater
Russell Norman
Fergus Henderson

(Elsewhere)
Chad Robertson
Nicolaus Bala and Cortney Burns
Russell Moore and Alleson Hopelain
David Tanis
Alice Waters
Rachel Alice Roddy
Rose Carrarini
Sara Midda
Mollie Katzen

Everyone who has come to Secret
Restaurant Portland and shown their
appreciation and encouragement.

To the residents of The Welling
Townhouse in North Bennington,
Vermont, during my time there. I
have been striving to keep up the
magic we shared ever since.

RECOMMENDED READING

The following books have had the greatest influence on my cooking. I hope you consider reading and learning from them as well.

Nicolaus Bala and Cortney Burns
Bar Tartine: Techniques & Recipes

Paul Bertolli
Chez Panisse Cooking

Rose Carrarini
Breakfast, Lunch, Tea: The Many Little Meals of Rose Bakery

Elizabeth David
Mediterranean Food
Italian Food
Summer Cooking

Judie Geise
The Northwest Kitchen: A Seasonal Cookbook

Fergus Henderson
The Complete Nose to Tail

Tom Hudgens
The Commonsense Kitchen

Mollie Katzen
Moosewood Cookbook
The Enchanted Broccoli Forest

Clare Lattin and Tom Hill
Ducksoup Cookbook: The Wisdom of Simple Cooking

Deborah Madison
Vegetable Literacy

Russell Moore and Allison Hopelain
This Is Camino

Russel Norman
Polpo: A Venetian Cookbook (of Sorts)
Spuntino: Comfort Food (New York Style)

Chad Robertson
Tartine Bread
Tartine Book No. 3

Rachel Alice Roddy
My Kitchen in Rome: Recipes and Notes on Italian Cooking

Nancy Singleton Hachisu
Japanese Farm Food
Preserving the Japanese Way

Nigel Slater
Eat
The Kitchen Diaries
Notes from the Larder
Tender
Ripe

David Tanis
One Good Dish
Heart of the Artichoke and Other Kitchen Journeys
A Platter of Figs and Other Recipes

Alice Waters
The Art of Simple Food I & II
Chez Panisse Pasta, Pizza & Calzone
Chez Panisse Vegetables
Chez Panisse Fruit
Chez Panisse Menu Cookbook

INDEX

CONVERSIONS

VOLUME			LENGTH		WEIGHT	
UNITED STATES	METRIC	IMPERIAL	UNITED STATES	METRIC	AVOIRDUPOIS	METRIC
¼ tsp.	1.25 ml		⅛ in.	3 mm	¼ oz.	7 g
½ tsp.	2.5 ml		¼ in.	6 mm	½ oz.	15 g
1 tsp.	5 ml		½ in.	1.25 cm	1 oz.	30 g
½ Tbsp.	7.5 ml		1 in.	2.5 cm	2 oz.	60 g
1 Tbsp.	15 ml		1 ft.	30 cm	3 oz.	90 g
⅛ c.	30 ml	1 fl. oz.			4 oz.	115 g
¼ c.	60 ml	2 fl. oz.			5 oz.	150 g
⅓ c.	80 ml	2.5 fl. oz.			6 oz.	175 g
½ c.	125 ml	4 fl. oz.			7 oz.	200 g
1 c.	250 ml	8 fl. oz.			8 oz. (½ lb.)	225 g
2 c. (1 pt.)	500 ml	16 fl. oz.			9 oz.	250 g
1 qt.	1 l	32 fl. oz.			10 oz.	300 g

TEMPERATURE				11 oz.	325 g
OVEN MARK	FAHRENHEIT	CELSIUS	GAS	12 oz.	350 g
Very cool	250–275	130–140	½–1	13 oz.	375 g
Cool	300	150	2	14 oz.	400 g
Warm	325	165	3	15 oz.	425 g
Moderate	350	175	4	16 oz. (1 lb.)	450 g
Moderately hot	375	190	5	1½ lb.	750 g
	400	200	6	2 lb.	900 g
Hot	425	220	7	2¼ lb.	1 kg
	450	230	8	3 lb.	1.4 kg
Very Hot	475	245	9	4 lb.	1.8 kg

To Sofie

Printed in China

Published by Sasquatch Books

21 20 19 18 17   9 8 7 6 5 4 3 2 1

FIRST EDITION PRODUCTION CREDITS

First published in 2015 as *Myrtlewood: Home Cooking from the Pacific Northwest*

Book design and lettering: Andrew Barton
Project manager and stylist: Kate Schweitzer
Project editor: Delphine Bedient
Assistant editors: Kate Schweitzer, Sofie Sherman-Burton, and Alleson Goldfinger
Styling by Kate Schweitzer

SECOND EDITION PRODUCTION CREDITS

Editor: Gary Luke
Production editor: Emma Reh
Design: Bryce de Flamand
Copyeditor: Dana Youlin

Garden photographs on page 3 © Nolan Calisch

Library of Congress Cataloging-in-Publication Data is available.

ISBN: 978-1-63217-141-2

Sasquatch Books
1904 Third Avenue, Suite 710
Seattle, WA 98101
(206) 467-4300
www.sasquatchbooks.com
custserv@sasquatchbooks.com

THE MYRTLEWOOD COOKBOOK is a book of seasonal home cooking. It was made in real time, in an apartment kitchen and backyard garden.

ANDREW BARTON is preschool teacher by day, cook by weeknight, weekend, and holiday. He is a graduate of Bennington College. Oregon is his home state. Secret Restaurant Portland has been active since 2010. SecretRestaurantPortland.com

---

PETER SCHWEITZER is a freelance photographer residing in Portland, Oregon. He is dedicated to capturing the mood of a moment, be that with a gathering of friends, the changing seasons, or the spaces around him. He continues to work on a documentary photo project reaching back to 2006. SchweitzerCreative.co

---

KATE SCHWEITZER is a visual artist and stylist. She can be found creating botanical drawings and tiny Instax photos, collecting flowers, or hiding in her library reading her favorite book. KateSchweitzer.co

---

Up north —
back to the pines,
the mushrooms,
the people,
the ideas

— Anton Chekhov